Practical Azure Functions

A Guide to Web, Mobile, and IoT Applications

Agus Kurniawan
Wely Lau

Apress®

Practical Azure Functions: A Guide to Web, Mobile, and IoT Applications

Agus Kurniawan
Fakultas Ilmu Komputer,
Universitas Indonesia, Depok, Indonesia

Wely Lau
Singapore, Singapore

ISBN-13 (pbk): 978-1-4842-5066-2
https://doi.org/10.1007/978-1-4842-5067-9

ISBN-13 (electronic): 978-1-4842-5067-9

Managing Director, Apress Media LLC: Welmoed Spahr
Acquisitions Editor: Natalie Pao
Development Editor: James Markham
Coordinating Editor: Jessica Vakili

Cover designed by eStudioCalamar

Cover image designed by Freepik (www.freepik.com)

Distributed to the book trade worldwide by Springer Science+Business Media New York, 233 Spring Street, 6th Floor, New York, NY 10013. Phone 1-800-SPRINGER, fax (201) 348-4505, e-mail orders-ny@springer-sbm.com, or visit www.springeronline.com. Apress Media, LLC is a California LLC and the sole member (owner) is Springer Science + Business Media Finance Inc (SSBM Finance Inc). SSBM Finance Inc is a **Delaware** corporation.

For information on translations, please e-mail rights@apress.com, or visit www.apress.com/rights-permissions.

Apress titles may be purchased in bulk for academic, corporate, or promotional use. eBook versions and licenses are also available for most titles. For more information, reference our Print and eBook Bulk Sales web page at www.apress.com/bulk-sales.

Any source code or other supplementary material referenced by the author in this book is available to readers on GitHub via the book's product page, located at www.apress.com/978-1-4842-5066-2. For more detailed information, please visit www.apress.com/source-code.

Printed on acid-free paper

To my wife, Ela and two children, Thariq and Zahra.
— Agus K

To my dearest wife Shirley and two little sweethearts, Aiden and Aileen. Without your support, I wouldn't have been able to complete this book.

To my parents, who raised me up to be who I am today. Genuine gratitude to you.

To my wonderful readers, thank you for taking your time to read this book. I sincerely hope this book elevates your knowledge on serverless computing to another level.
— Wely Lau, 2019

Table of Contents

About the Authors

Agus Kurniawan is a lecturer, IT consultant, and author. He has 15 years of experience working on various software and hardware development projects, delivering materials in training and workshops, and doing technical writing. He has been awarded the Microsoft Most Valuable Professional (MVP) award 14 years in a row.

Agus is a lecturer and researcher in the field of networking and security systems as part of the Faculty of Computer Science at Universitas Indonesia, Indonesia. Currently, he is pursuing a PhD in computer science at the Freie Universität Berlin, Germany. He can be reached on Twitter at **@agusk2010**.

Wely Lau is a developer, architect, trainer, consultant, technical writer, and technology lover.

With the grant of the ASEAN Graduate Scholarship, Wely obtained his MS in information systems from Nanyang Technological University. He currently works as a cloud solution architect on the Azure application development platform for Microsoft Asia Pacific.

In his spare time, he writes a blog, delivers presentations, and participates in the online community. His passion in driving Microsoft technologies, especially Azure, resulted in him being awarded the first Windows Azure MVP in Southeast Asia.

Wely can be reached by e-mail at `wely.lau@gmail.com`.

About the Technical Reviewer

Mayur Tendulkar is technology solutions professional who works at Microsoft in Singapore, helping people with technology. Previously he was a program manager on the Xamarin team at Microsoft, working in Pune, India. Before joining Microsoft, he was awarded the Microsoft Most Valuable Professional for Windows development and worked as a developer evangelist with Xamarin. He has been writing mobile applications since the days of Windows Mobile 5.0 and loves everything mobile and cloud these days. You can find him talking at conferences, at user groups, and on various social channels. His coordinates are @mayur_Tendulkar and mayur-tendulkar on Git. You can follow his thoughts on his blog: http://mayurtendulkar.com.

CHAPTER 1

Introduction to Azure Functions

Azure Functions is a Microsoft Azure service that provides a serverless solution, enabling developers to address their business problems efficiently. In this chapter, we will start by demystifying the serverless concept. Subsequently, we will explore Azure Functions and show how to set up the development environment. Then, we will show how to develop a simple program with Azure Functions.

The following topics are covered:

- An overview of serverless computing

- Introduction to Azure Functions

- How to set up the development environment

- How to develop a simple program using Azure Functions

- How to use the Azure portal

© Agus Kurniawan, Wely Lau 2019
A. Kurniawan and W. Lau, *Practical Azure Functions*,
https://doi.org/10.1007/978-1-4842-5067-9_1

An Overview of Serverless Computing

Serverless computing, or in short *serverless*, is yet another buzzword in the computing industry that has been very popular in recent years.

There are several characteristics and benefits of serverless. First, the term *serverless* doesn't mean that there are no servers. There are certainly servers involved; however, they are being abstracted. That means developers do not need to worry about the server provisioning, software patching, and scaling. It will all be taken care of by the serverless platform. This enables developers to focus more on writing code to solve business problems.

In addition, the code that you deploy to the serverless platform will be executed based on a specific event. Here are some examples:

- You can use a timer trigger to clear a temporary table in a database every Friday at 2 p.m.

- You can use a queue trigger when a new order is added to a queue.

- You can use an HTTP web trigger when an HTTP-based endpoint is being invoked by a browser or client.

Another benefit of serverless computing is the subsecond billing model. The serverless computing options offered by the major cloud platforms typically have competitive billing models, and you pay only for the resources that you utilize.

Does that sound like platform as a service (PaaS) or infrastructure as a service (IaaS)? It sort of is, but at a finer-grained level.

When you provision a PaaS or IaaS resource (such as a virtual machine [VM]), you are billed for the duration of VM uptime or running state. Whether the VM is 10 percent or 50 percent or 90 percent utilized, you pay the same price, because that entire VM is technically rented to you.

By contrast, with serverless, you will be billed only for the resource execution time and resource consumption. That is because your code will be run on a pool of available servers, assigned by the serverless platform.

The benefit of this is a better price point and cost efficiency.

Introduction to Azure Functions

As mentioned, Azure Functions is an Azure service from Microsoft that provides serverless solutions for running small pieces of code. When using the service, you can focus on writing code to solve business problems without worrying too much about the whole platform or infrastructure. Therefore, it can significantly accelerate your development time. You can read more about Microsoft Azure Functions at `https://azure.microsoft. com/en-us/services/functions/`, as shown in Figure 1-1.

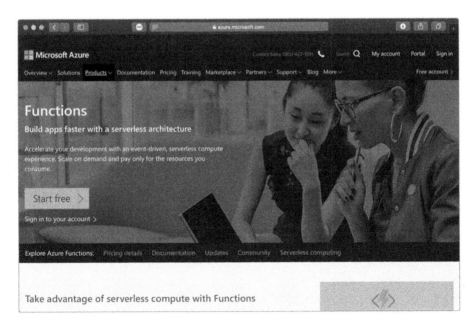

Figure 1-1. *Official web page for Azure Functions*

Supported Languages

Currently, there are three officially supported languages in Azure Functions: C#, JavaScript, and F#. However, there are other languages that are expected to be supported in the future such as Java, Python, PHP, and more.

You can find the list of supported programming languages at `https://docs.microsoft.com/en-us/azure/azure-functions/supported-languages`.

Function Runtime

The Azure Functions runtime defines the fundamental way your function will run on top of the platform. There are two versions of the Azure Functions runtime: 1.x and 2.x. The following are the main differences between the two:

- Runtime 1.x only supports development on the Windows platform because it was built on the .NET Framework.

- Runtime 2.x supports development across platforms, including Windows, Linux, and macOS, as it was built on top of .NET Core.

To learn more about the considerations when choosing the runtime version as well as the migration process, visit `https://docs.microsoft.com/en-us/azure/azure-functions/functions-versions`.

Why Azure Functions?

We've already discussed the general benefits of serverless computing. There are additional competitive advantages of Azure Functions, listed here:

- **Fully open source:** Azure Functions is open source, which enables the community to contribute their ideas or file issues to try to improve the product. You can find the source code of the runtime/host, samples, command-line tools, templates, and UI here: `https://github.com/Azure/Azure-Functions`.

- **Inherits the Azure platform capabilities:** As one of the important services, Azure Functions naturally inherits tons of capabilities from Azure. This includes a multiregion presence around the globe, security, compliance and certification, platform operation, and many other aspects.

- **Integration with other services:** Azure Functions has so many built-in integrations with services including Azure services (such as Azure Storage, the SQL database, Cosmos DB, etc.) and external services (such as SendGrid e-mail services, Twilio SMS services, and even external files).

- **Community and official support:** From a community support perspective, developers can easily find documentation, sample codes, and resources on the Internet.

  - **StackOverflow:** `https://stackoverflow.com/questions/tagged/azure-functions`

  - **MSDN Forum:** `https://social.msdn.microsoft.com/Forums/azure/en-US/home?forum=azure functions`

  - **Raising issue in GitHub:** `https://github.com/Azure/Azure-Functions/issues`

Customers can raise an official commercial support ticket for Microsoft, as discussed here: `https://docs.microsoft.com/en-us/azure/azure-supportability/how-to-create-azure-support-request`.

Setting Up the Development Environment

Though you could write and deploy your function code directly on the Azure portal, developing and testing your functions locally provides higher productivity and convenience.

Depending on your language and operating system preference, here are several popular ways to develop functions with Azure Functions:

- Command prompt and terminal (supports C#, C# Script, JavaScript)

- Visual Studio Code (supports C#, C# Script, JavaScript)

- Visual Studio 2019 or 2019 (supports C# only)

Figure 1-2 illustrates how you as a developer will be able to access Azure Functions through the previously mentioned techniques.

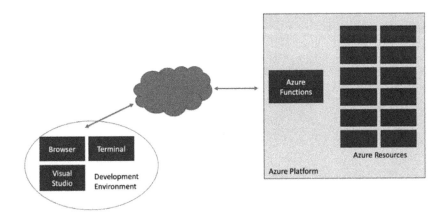

Figure 1-2. *Development environment and interaction with Azure Functions*

In addition, you can use Application Insights to perform application monitoring, which will be discussed in more detail in Chapter 9.

You can find more information including how to install these packages and tools at `https://docs.microsoft.com/en-us/azure/azure-functions/functions-develop-local`.

You will learn how to develop Azure Functions programs in this book primarily using Visual Studio 2019 with Visual C#. Microsoft provides a project template for Azure Functions in Visual Studio 2019. From the welcome screen, choose New Project. Type **function** in the search bar, and you should see the Azure Functions project template, as shown in Figure 1-3.

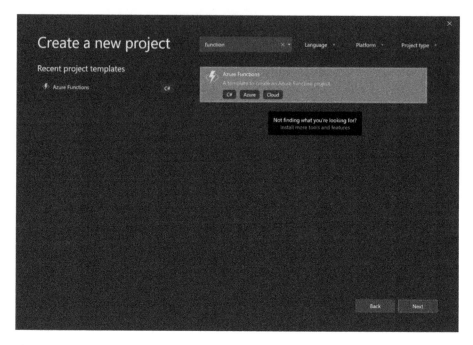

Figure 1-3. Project template for Azure Functions in Visual Studio 2019

Building a Simple Azure Functions Program

In this section, you will build your first simple program with Azure Functions. You also will use the existing Azure Functions template for this demo. Then, you will call the program from a browser. To implement this demo, you should have an active Microsoft Azure account. Microsoft also provides a trial for Microsoft Azure, which can be found at `https://azure.microsoft.com/en-us/offers/ms-azr-0044p/`.

Let's get started!

Creating a Project

First, let's create a project for Azure Functions using the Azure portal. You can access it at `https://portal.azure.com/`. Technically, you can use any browser to access the Azure portal. After logging on to your Azure account, you can start creating a resource with Azure Functions. Click the "Create a resource" item, as shown in Figure 1-4.

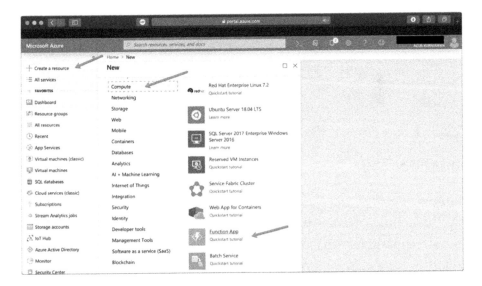

Figure 1-4. *Creating a new Azure Functions resource*

Select Function App, as shown in Figure 1-4. Subsequently, you will see a Function App form, as shown in Figure 1-5. Fill in all the fields to create a function app.

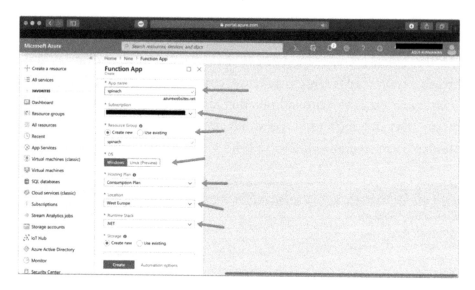

Figure 1-5. *Filling in the Functions App form*

Function App

Think of a *function app* like a container that hosts the execution of one or more functions. This means all the functions that you create within this function app will inherit the same configuration such as the operating system, hosting plan, runtime stack, and so on.

Operating System

You can choose to run your function app on either the Windows or Linux operating system (Linux is currently in Preview). We will choose Windows in this example.

Hosting Plan

The hosting plan defines how your function app will eventually run.

Choosing the Consumption Plan enables your function app to run on the pool of shared resources among all other tenants and obviously with the appropriate security measurements and segregation in place.

Your function app will be scaled automatically by Azure when the load increases or decreases. You will be billed only for the execution and resource consumption when your code is executed. Therefore, you can consider this option to be truly serverless.

You can also choose to deploy your function app on an existing App Service Plan. Because you define the size of your App Service Plan (the number of instances and the size of each instance), the resource function app will be dedicated to you. However, you will be responsible for scaling the plan. With this option, you will be billed based on the App Service Plan, regardless of how many times your code executes. Another benefit of the App Service Plan is that it enables you to access some additional features such as virtual network (vnet) connectivity and the Always On feature, which allows you to control a cold start. These features are not available in the Consumption Plan.

At the time of this writing, Microsoft has just introduced a new plan in Preview mode named Premium Plan. The main objective of introducing this option is to provide better performance (of each instance size) as well as more predictable pricing. You can learn more about the Premium Plan at `https://docs.microsoft.com/en-us/azure/azure-functions/functions-scale#premium-plan`.

For the example in this chapter, we will choose the Consumption Plan.

Runtime Stack

The runtime stack defines the preinstalled runtime environment that will run your code in the language of your choice such as .NET, JavaScript, or Java. For the example in this chapter, we will select .NET.

You can fill in all the required fields including Resource Group and Storage.

When you're done, click Create. You will then have an Azure portal that shows your Azure function app. You can check whether the Azure function app is already created. Figure 1-6 shows our function app, called *spinach*. You can see that the function app creation wizard generates four Azure resources.

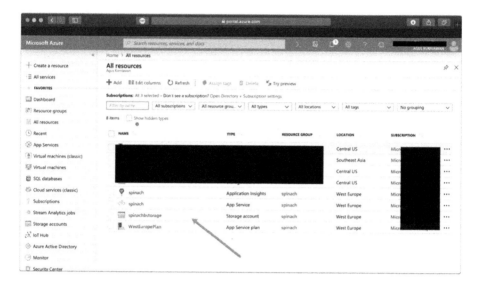

Figure 1-6. *A function app was created*

Next, you can create a function on the function app.

Creating a function in a function app

To create a function, you should go to the Function Apps dashboard by clicking your function app.

After clicking your function app, you should see the Function Apps dashboard, as shown in Figure 1-7. There are three types of apps in your function app: functions, proxies, and slots. As of this writing, the slots feature is in Preview mode.

Figure 1-7. *Azure Function Apps dashboard*

If you click Functions, you should get a list of functions that you have created. You can see this in Figure 1-8.

Figure 1-8. *A list of functions in Azure Functions*

For the demo purposes, we will use a project template. Select the "HTTP trigger" template by clicking the + icon to the right of Functions (as shown in Figure 1-9).

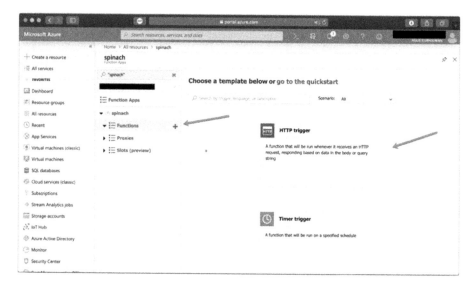

Figure 1-9. *Creating a new Azure Functions project based on a template*

You will get the form shown in Figure 1-10. Fill in all the required fields. Select Function as the authentication level. When you're done, click the Create button.

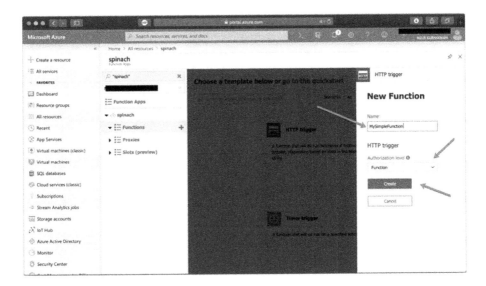

Figure 1-10. *Filling in a name*

After clicking the Create button, you should get the form shown in Figure 1-11. You will see some sample code from the project template (HTTP trigger). You can also edit this program directly in a web editor.

15

Figure 1-11. *Code in the template*

Now you are ready to run the program.

Running the Application

You can run the program by clicking the Run button. You should get the dialog shown in Figure 1-12. Copy this URL, add &name=xxx to it, and paste the URL into another browser tab.

Figure 1-12. *Getting a copy of the URL*

If you succeed, you should get a response from the server. For instance, we set name=agusk, so you can see our program output in Figure 1-13.

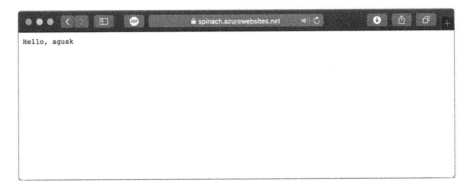

Figure 1-13. *Accessing an Azure Functions application from a browser*

Try changing it to name=??, with ?? as your own name. Then, visit the URL in a browser.

Accessing Azure Functions in the Azure Portal

Azure Functions provides some features and tools to manage its service. If you open the Azure dashboard, you should see some resources (Figure 1-14).

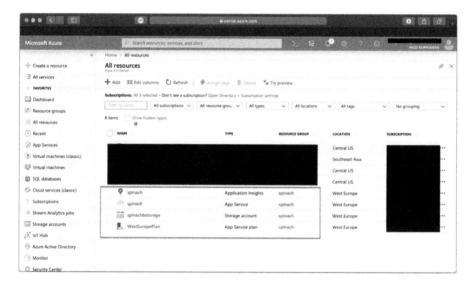

Figure 1-14. *All these resources are related to Azure Functions*

If you want to open a function app, open a resource by clicking App Services. Then, you should get the form shown in Figure 1-15. There are two tabs on this form, Overview and "Platform features."

The "Platform features" tab consists of configuration settings, tools, and monitoring settings. You can configure a custom domain and manage authentication. You also can work with some tools by following the links.

Figure 1-15. *Several features and tools for a function app*

If you are familiar with Azure App Service, you will notice that its platform features are similar. This is because Azure Functions is hosted on the same underlying technologies as Azure App Service.

You will explore these features in the upcoming chapters, getting details and working through various scenarios.

Comparing Azure Functions to Logic Apps

While the main topic of this book is Azure Functions, it's worthwhile to mention another serverless offering named Logic Apps. You can think of Azure Functions as a serverless code platform, while Logic Apps is a serverless workflow-based platform suitable for integration scenarios. There is very little (in fact almost none) code required while authoring a Logic Apps solution. Logic Apps comes with a visual designer, which can be accessed from the Azure portal, as shown in Figure 1-16, or a tool such as Visual Studio.

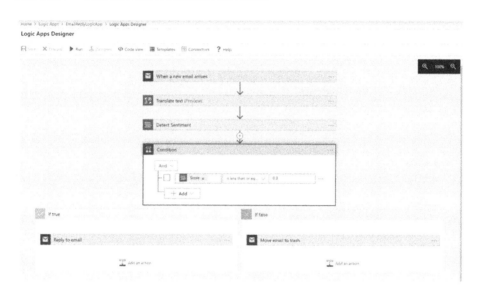

Figure 1-16. *Visual designer of Logic Apps*

Table 1-1 compares Azure Functions to Logic Apps.

Table 1-1. *Comparison of Azure Functions and Logic Apps*

	Azure Functions	**Logic Apps**
Authoring style	Code-based with multiple languages	Workflow-based visual designer
Connectors	Minimum; supports mostly Azure services in triggers and bindings; some external connectors for output bindings	More than 200 connectors from Azure-based to Microsoft ecosystems to third parties and more
Deployment model	Can be deployed as the Consumption Plan or a dedicated plan in an app service environment	Can be deployed as the Consumption Plan or a dedicated plan in an integrated service environment
Runtime	Open source and can be deployed locally or also available in Azure	Available only in the Azure cloud

Note that you can invoke Azure Functions programs from the Logic Apps designer, as shown in Figure 1-17.

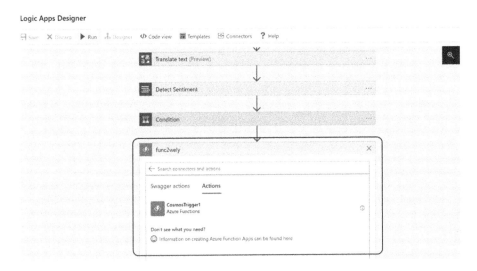

Figure 1-17. *Integrating Azure Functions with Logic Apps*

Summary

In this chapter, we started with the concept of serverless computing. You then learned what Azure Functions is. You also developed a simple Azure Functions program from a template. We subsequently compared Azure Functions to Logic Apps.

In the next chapter, you will focus on Azure Functions programming with some scenarios.

CHAPTER 2

Azure Functions Programming

This chapter discusses the programming model of Azure Functions and enables you to increase your development productivity.

Exploring the Azure Functions Programming Model

While Azure Functions provides some serverless benefits, one of its unique features is its programming model, which simplifies the way developers write code through *bindings*.

Integration with other services (regardless of whether they're within Azure or external to it) is common and critically important. As such, triggers and bindings allow developers to access other services more efficiently while writing less code.

Triggers

As you can tell from the name, a *trigger* defines how a function will be executed based on a specific event. The trigger could be an HTTP request, a timer that is set to run every five minutes, or even a new message that is enqueued.

You can have only one trigger per function.

© Agus Kurniawan, Wely Lau 2019
A. Kurniawan and W. Lau, *Practical Azure Functions*,
https://doi.org/10.1007/978-1-4842-5067-9_2

Input Bindings

In the event that your code needs to process or access supplementary data from other services, *input* can really simplify the way you code.

Take the example of reading a blob text file from an Azure Blob Storage account. Traditionally, you would need to use the Azure Blob Storage SDK or the REST API (depending on your choice of programming languages). This can take 12 to 20 lines of code, including the instantiation of `CloudStorageAccount`, `CloudBlobClient`, `CloudBlobContainer`, and so on.

An input binding can achieve this much more easily in just five lines in the binding config file.

You can have more than one input binding in a function.

Output Bindings

As you can tell from the name, an *output* defines how you want to produce the result that you've written in your code.

You can have more than one output binding in a function.

Figure 2-1 and Figure 2-2 illustrate how triggers and bindings are defined in both configuration files (`function.json`) and the actual function code (`run.csx`).

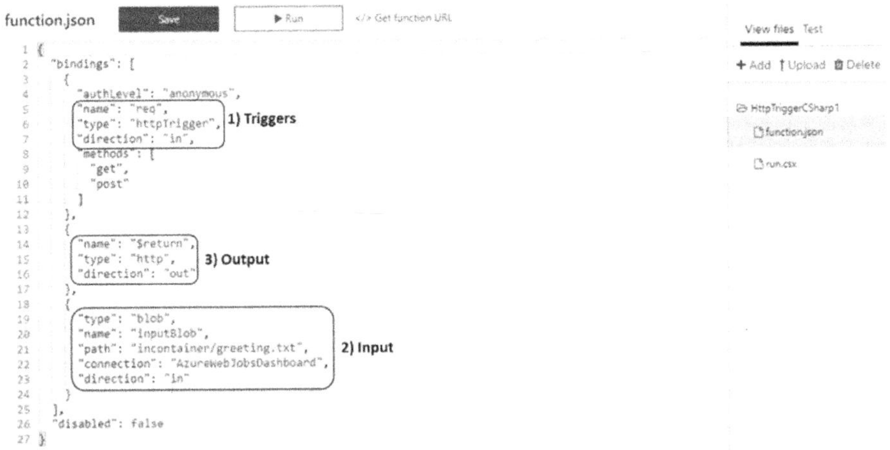

```
function.json       Save          ▶ Run         </> Get function URL                              View files  Test

1  {                                                                                          + Add  ↑Upload  🗑 Delete
2    "bindings": [
3      {                                                                                      🗁 HttpTriggerCSharp1
4        "authLevel": "anonymous",                                                               ↳ function.json
5        "name": "req",
6        "type": "httpTrigger",    1) Triggers                                                  🗋 run.csx
7        "direction": "in",
8        "methods": [
9          "get",
10         "post"
11       ]
12     },
13     {
14       "name": "$return",
15       "type": "http",       3) Output
16       "direction": "out"
17     },
18     {
19       "type": "blob",
20       "name": "inputBlob",
21       "path": "incontainer/greeting.txt",    2) Input
22       "connection": "AzureWebJobsDashboard",
23       "direction": "in"
24     }
25   ],
26   "disabled": false
27 }
```

Figure 2-1. *An example of a function configuration file (function.json)*

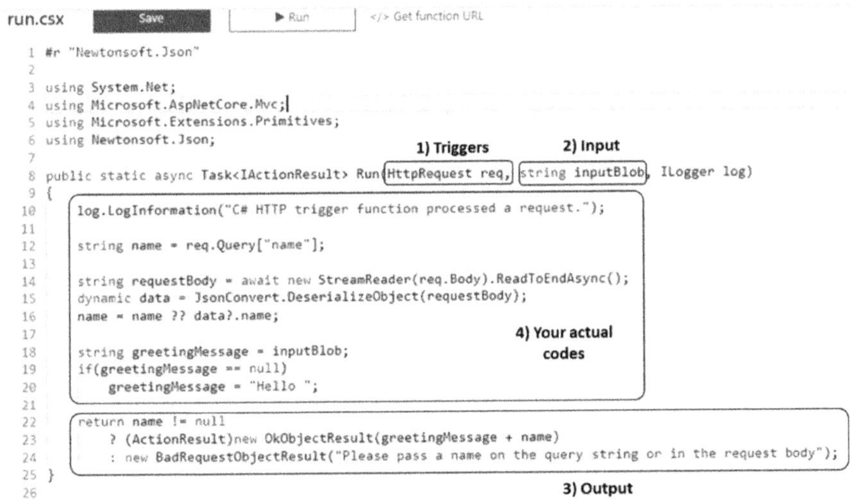

```
run.csx        Save          ▶ Run         </> Get function URL

1  #r "Newtonsoft.Json"
2
3  using System.Net;
4  using Microsoft.AspNetCore.Mvc;
5  using Microsoft.Extensions.Primitives;
6  using Newtonsoft.Json;
7                                         1) Triggers        2) Input
8  public static async Task<IActionResult> Run(HttpRequest req, string inputBlob, ILogger log)
9  {
10     log.LogInformation("C# HTTP trigger function processed a request.");
11
12     string name = req.Query["name"];
13
14     string requestBody = await new StreamReader(req.Body).ReadToEndAsync();
15     dynamic data = JsonConvert.DeserializeObject(requestBody);
16     name = name ?? data?.name;
17                                              4) Your actual
18     string greetingMessage = inputBlob;            codes
19     if(greetingMessage == null)
20         greetingMessage = "Hello ";
21
22     return name != null
23         ? (ActionResult)new OkObjectResult(greetingMessage + name)
24         : new BadRequestObjectResult("Please pass a name on the query string or in the request body");
25 }
26                                                 3) Output
```

Figure 2-2. *An example of an actual function (run.csx)*

You can define triggers and bindings in several ways in the Azure Functions programming model. The previous sample uses C# Script (`.csx`). Obviously, the code will differ when you use C#, JavaScript, or another programming language. For more details, you can see other variations here: `https://docs.microsoft.com/en-us/azure/azure-functions/functions-triggers-bindings#example-trigger-and-binding`.

Creating Functions from a Template or the Quickstart

In this section, you will explore how to create a function from a template and the quickstart process.

Creating Functions from a Template

As you learned in Chapter 1, when you click the + icon to add a function, you will see the list of function templates based on language and scenario, as shown in Figure 2-3.

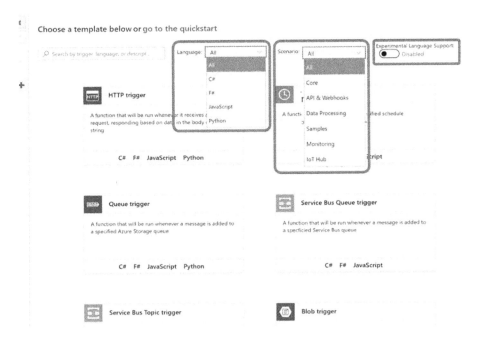

Figure 2-3. *List of templates*

These templates allow developers to create functions by filtering the languages (C#, F#, JavaScript, and so on) or scenarios (Core, API & Webhooks, IoT Hub, etc.). You can also choose to enable the experimental language support for more language options.

Creating Functions from the Quickstart

As you can see, with more than 60 templates, there are many combinations that you can choose from. You can also choose from the quickstart menu for a simpler view by clicking the "go to the quickstart" link. This will enable you to choose only two steps (the scenario and then the language), as shown in Figure 2-4.

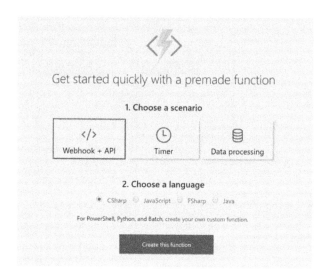

Figure 2-4. *Creating functions from the quickstart menu*

Using Webhook + API

Let's explore Webhook + API, as this is one of the most popular options when using Azure Functions. This option simply generates an HTTP endpoint, and your code will be executed when the endpoint URL is invoked.

As shown in Figure 2-4, choose Webhook + API from the scenario options, then select CSharp from the language options, and finally click the "Create this function" button.

You will notice that the function with the default name HttpTrigger1 (along with several files) will be created (see Figure 2-5). This is similar to what you saw in Figure 2-2.

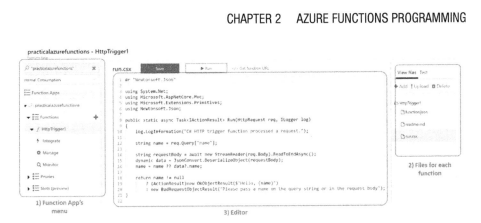

Figure 2-5. *Azure Functions template created with Webhook + API*

- The left menu displays a list of resources (including functions) within your function app.

- The right menu shows files for each function. function.json is the function's configuration file, while run.csx is your actual function code.

- The editor in the center displays sample code for your function. Notice that the editor will load the file according to your selection on the right.

Integrate Menu

Let's explore the Integrate menu, which is right below your function name, in the left menu. The upper section allows you to define the triggers, inputs, and outputs of the function. Figure 2-6 shows how the associated information is displayed.

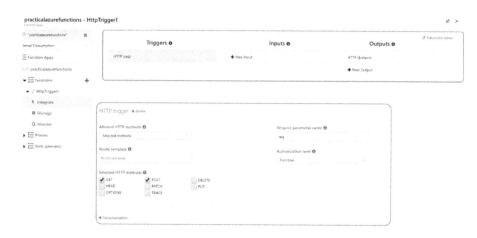

Figure 2-6. *Integrate menu in an HTTP trigger*

Because you chose Webhook + API in the quickstart menu, the Azure portal automatically populates the HTTP trigger for you. You can modify the HTTP trigger accordingly as follows:

- Choosing all or selected HTTP methods (GET, POST, DELETE, and so on)

- Defining a route template

- Defining a request parameter (default name required)

- Setting the authorization level, which includes the following:

    - **Anonymous:** Anybody can invoke this function without having to present any key.

    - **Function:** You can invoke this function by presenting the key at the function level, which means each function will have its own key.

    - **Admin:** You can invoke this function only with an admin (master) key.

Click + New Input in the upper part, and you will see several input binding options. Choose Azure Blob Storage and click Select (see Figure 2-7).

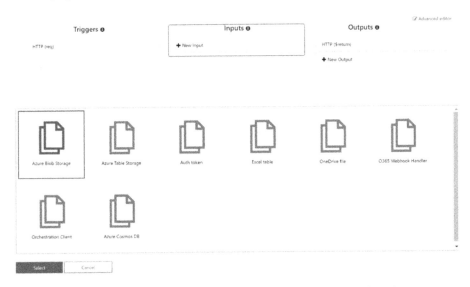

Figure 2-7. *Choosing Azure Blob Storage as the input binding*

If you encounter a warning regarding the Azure Blob Storage input extension not being installed, simply click Install. After a few moments, you should be able to use this Blob Storage input binding (Figure 2-8).

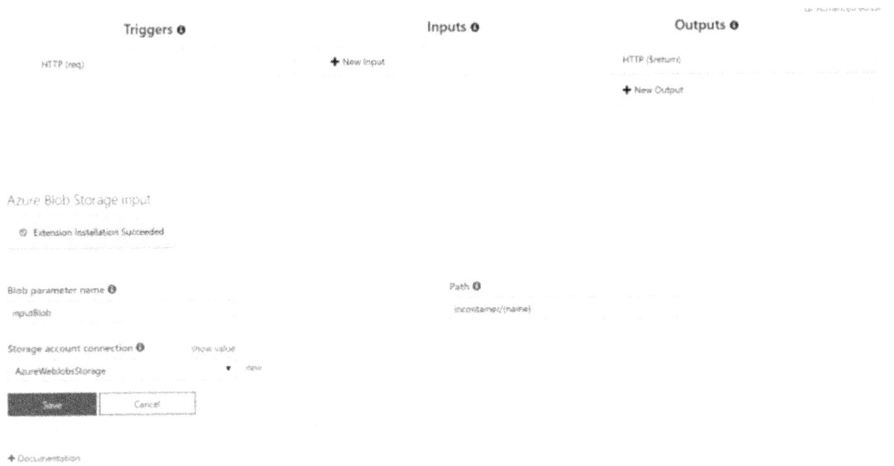

Figure 2-8. *Blob Storage input binding details*

You can leave the storage account as it is or choose your preferred storage account to fetch the blob from. In our case, we already prepared a storage account, container, and blob in the form of a text file, as shown in Figure 2-9.

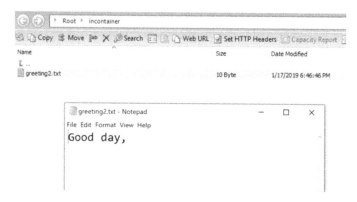

Figure 2-9. *Preparing the storage account, container, and blob*

The path defines the blob storage container and the blob name. In this example, change it to `incontainer/greeting2.txt`.

`BlobParameterName` is the parameter name that will be used in your function code. You can just leave it set to `inputBlob`. You can click Save after that. Next, let's explore the outputs.

As you can see in Figure 2-10, the Webhook + API template provides HTTP($return) under Outputs, which you can click to find out more details. You can also click + New Output since the output binding allows you to have more than one output.

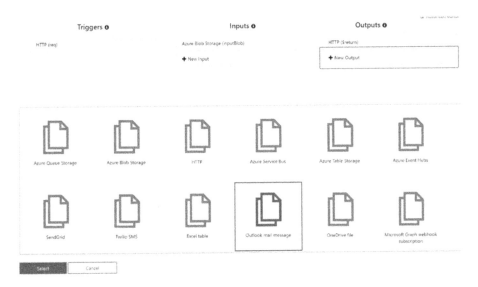

Figure 2-10. *Output bindings*

The changes you perform in the user interface (including for triggers, inputs, and outputs) are reflected in the function.json configuration file. You can view this file through the "Advanced editor" link at the top-right corner, or you can navigate to the function.json file, as shown in Figure 2-5.

Before running and testing the function, make sure to update your code in the run.csx file, as shown in Figure 2-2. As you can guess, this example will display the greeting you specified in your blob storage account. However, if there isn't any message found in the blob, it will display the default greeting "Hello."

Manage Menu

Let's take a step back and further explore the Manage menu for your HttpTrigger1 function by clicking Manage (Figure 2-11). This menu lets you do the following:

- Enable and disable the function state

- Delete the function

- Manage the keys of function (including the function-level keys as well as the host- or master-level keys)

Figure 2-11. *Manage menu on each function*

Use Cases of Webhook + API

There many use cases that you can develop with this template, such as the following:

- Developing an HTTP API endpoint to listen for a webhook callback

- Serving as a middle-layer HTTP API for a web front end such as Angular

- Serving as a middle-layer HTTP API for a mobile application

We will discuss these use cases in more detail in the upcoming chapters.

Setting Up a Timer-Based Function

The timer-based function is another popular template. The idea is to execute a function on a specific scheduled defined as a CRON expression. Azure Functions makes use of the NCrontab library for the CRON interpretation.

Using a CRON Expression in NCrontab

A CRON expression is a simple yet powerful way to specify a recurring time in a string containing five or six characters separated with spaces. You can learn more about the CRON expression in the examples shown at `https://github.com/atifaziz/NCrontab`.

Figure 2-12 explains the CRON format for NCrontab.

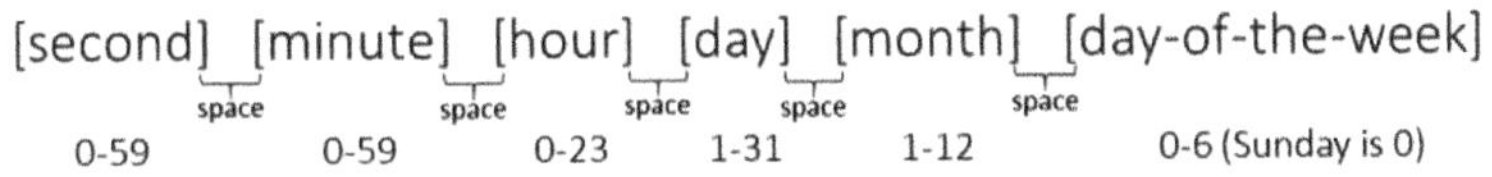

[second] [minute] [hour] [day] [month] [day-of-the-week]
         space   space   space   space   space
0-59   0-59   0-23   1-31   1-12   0-6 (Sunday is 0)

Figure 2-12.   *CRON format in timer-based Azure Functions*

Table 2-1 shows several examples of CRON expressions.

Table 2-1.   *Example CRON Expressions*

Number	CRON Expression	Meaning
1	*/10 * * * *	Run every ten seconds
2	0 0 10 * * *	Run at 10 every day
3	0 15 11 * * 1	Run at 11:15 every Monday
4	0 */5 22-23 * * 1-5	Run every five minutes between 10 p.m. and 11 p.m. only on weekdays

Notice that you can set the schedule with a simple or a complicated expression.

Creating a Timer-Based Function

Now that you understand how CRON expressions work, let's start creating a timer-based function. To do that, you can use either the quickstart or the template option, as discussed earlier in this chapter.

Figure 2-13 shows how to create a timer trigger function by using the template option.

Figure 2-13. *Creating a timer-based function*

Give the function a name and define the schedule based on a CRON expression, which you learned about earlier. As you can tell, the template autogenerates 0 */5 * * * * in the Schedule box, which means run the function every five minutes. Change the expression to */10 * * * * * to run this function every ten seconds.

Click Create; then the code editor screen will be shown. Expand the bottom section to display the log (see Figure 2-14).

Figure 2-14. *Logs in timer-based trigger function*

The provided sample code just performs logging with a description of "C# Timer trigger function executed on TIME," on the schedule you defined earlier, which is every ten seconds.

Exploring Use Cases for Timer-Based Functions

Timer-based functions are useful for use cases such as the following:

- Clearing temporary or log tables on a certain frequency

- Performing calculations or processing information from a master table and outputting to a calculated or summary table

- Sending a report e-mail at the end of every month

Messaging with the Azure Service Bus Queue Trigger Template

The asynchronous architecture of Azure Functions enables developers to create more robust solutions without having to be online all the time. As a matter of fact, in today world, many factors such as network and hardware are considered unreliable.

Therefore, you should design resilient solutions that can self-recover when an unexpected event occurs. Messaging and queuing systems play an important part in this architecture.

Azure Functions provides several varieties of this template including the following:

- Azure Queue Storage Trigger

- Azure Service Bus Queue Trigger

- Azure Service Bus Topic Trigger

- Azure Blob Storage Trigger

- Azure Event Hub Trigger

- Azure Cosmos DB Trigger

Although each of these templates uses different Azure services, the concept of a trigger is similar in each template: when an item (which could be a message, a blob, or a record) appears, trigger the function.

In this section, you'll learn how to use the Azure Service Bus queue with Azure Functions. Azure Service Bus offers reliable cloud-based messaging as a service. The two main capabilities are queues (for FIFO message delivery from a producer to one or more competing consumers) and topics/subscriptions (for the publish/subscribe model).

Let's learn more about how to integrate the Azure Service Bus queue with Azure Functions. Take the following scenario as an example:

- A new sales order is added into a queue.

- The new sales order will be processed by the Azure Functions function.

- A notification e-mail will be sent once the sales order is processed.

Creating an Azure Service Bus

First, you'll need to create a service bus namespace, which is a scoping container for Azure's messaging component.

To do that, click the "+ Create a resource" button in the left menu of the Azure portal (`https://portal.azure.com`); then type **Service Bus**, click Create, and fill in the details, as shown in Figure 2-15.

Figure 2-15. *Creating an Azure Service Bus namespace*

Once the Azure Service Bus namespace is created, you'll need to create a queue. To do that, click + Queue and fill in the queue name and details (Figure 2-16). In our example, the Azure Service Bus namespace is called **practicalazurefunctionssb**, and we named the queue **order**. You can leave the other fields (such as "Max queue size," etc.) at their defaults.

Figure 2-16. *Creating an Azure Service Bus queue*

The next step is for you to send a message to the order queue. To do that, you can do either of the following:

- Use the Azure Service Bus Explorer tools: `https://github.com/paolosalvatori/ServiceBusExplorer/releases`.

- Use the Service Bus SDK. This example shows a .NET SDK: `https://docs.microsoft.com/en-us/azure/service-bus-messaging/service-bus-dotnet-get-started-with-queues#send-messages-to-the-queue`.

Figure 2-17 shows how to use the Service Bus Explorer tool to enqueue the message "10 unit of Surface Laptop."

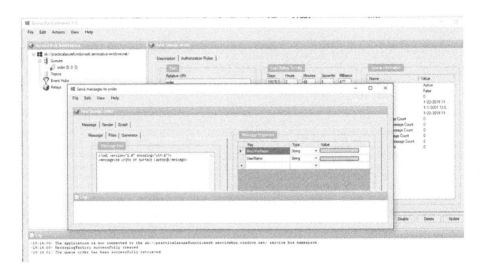

Figure 2-17. *Service Bus Explorer tool*

Creating an Azure Functions Function with a Service Bus Queue Trigger

Click the + button and choose "Azure Service Bus Queue trigger" for the template (Figure 2-18). If you get a warning message indicating that the extension isn't installed, just click Install and wait for a few moments.

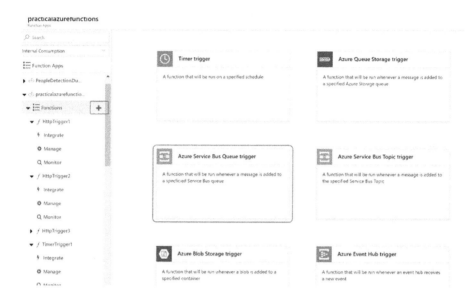

Figure 2-18. *Creating an Azure Service Bus queue trigger function*

Subsequently, you will need to fill in the details for the Azure Service Bus details (Figure 2-19). Follow these steps:

1. Name your function. As you can see, the default name is ServiceBusQueueTrigger1.

2. It's important to determine which Azure Service Bus account to use. As such, click New and browse to the Azure Service Bus namespace you created earlier; then click Select. In the event your service bus is in a different Azure subscription, you should choose Custom.

3. For the queue name, make sure you enter the queue name you created earlier. In this case, ours is called **order**. Then click Create.

Figure 2-19. *Filling in the details of the Azure Service Bus queue trigger function*

After a few moments, you will see that the function is successfully created, and you will be routed to the code editor page with run.csx open. Expand the bottom log section and take a closer look at the log message, as shown in Figure 2-20.

Figure 2-20. *Logs in the Azure Service Bus queue trigger function*

Preparing SendGrid

SendGrid is a popular e-mail service provider. To register for a free trial account, go to `https://sendgrid.com/free/`.

Once you have a SendGrid account, create an API key (Figure 2-21), making note of it and securing it properly as you may not want to view it again for security reasons.

Figure 2-21. *Creating API keys in SendGrid*

Adding an E-mail Address as an Output Binding

Navigate to the Integrate menu under your Azure Service Bus queue trigger function, click + New Output, and select SendGrid. Select the "Use function return value" check box and fill in e-mail addresses in the "from address" and "to address" boxes (Figure 2-22). In the SendGrid API Key App Setting field, click New and fill in the API key with the value you copied in the previous section. You can leave "Message subject" and Message Text empty as you will fill them in programmatically later in your function code. Click Save to accept the changes.

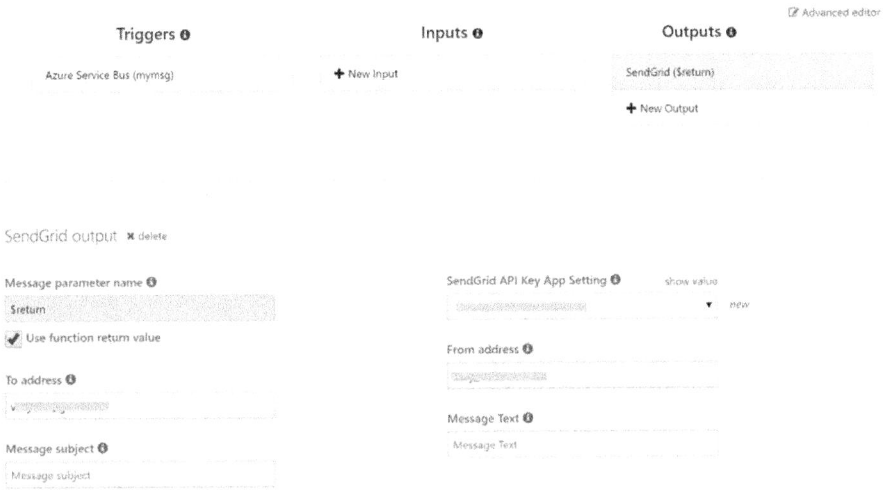

Figure 2-22. *SendGrid output binding*

Updating the Azure Function Code

Navigate to your function code editor by clicking your function name; in our case, this is ServiceBusQueueTrigger1. Replace the current code with the code snippet in Listing 2-1 and click Save.

Listing 2-1. Sending E-mail with SendGrid When a Message Is Enqueued

```
#r "SendGrid"
using System;
using System.Threading.Tasks;
using SendGrid.Helpers.Mail;
using Microsoft.Azure.WebJobs.Host;
```

```
public static SendGridMessage Run(string myQueueItem, ILogger log)
{
    SendGridMessage message = new SendGridMessage()
    {
        Subject = "Order received on " + DateTime.Now.ToString()
    };

    message.AddContent("text/plain", $"Hi there, we've received
    your order. We'll let you know agian when your order is on
    its way. Order: {myQueueItem}");

    return message;
}
```

You started by importing SendGrid as an external library since it's not part of the standard .NET/C# library. Subsequently, you will have four using directives including SendGrid.Helpers.Mail, as you'll be using some of the class in your code. In the Run method, you then create a SendGridMessage class and fill in the subject and message accordingly, before returning the SendGrid's message as a return value.

Testing the Service Bus Queue Trigger Function

Since this is an Azure Service Bus queue trigger function, you'll need to enqueue a message in the Azure Service Bus queue. As discussed, you can use either the Service Bus Explorer or the SDK to enqueue a message. Figure 2-23 shows how we enqueued a message containing "4 Unit of Surface Book 2" with the Service Bus Explorer.

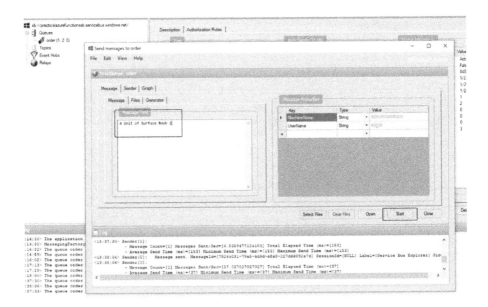

Figure 2-23. *Sending a message in the Service Bus Explorer*

Before hitting the Start button, navigate back to your Azure portal, particularly the function code editor that is displaying run.csx. Expand the Log section at the bottom.

Go back to your Service Bus Explorer and hit the Start button to start the enqueue. Immediately, navigate back to your Azure portal and notice the log. If everything works well, you should see the logs, as shown in Figure 2-24.

```
run.csx        Save          ▶ Run
   1  #r "SendGrid"
   2  using System;
   3  using System.Threading.Tasks;
   4  using SendGrid.Helpers.Mail;
   5  using Microsoft.Azure.WebJobs.Host;
   6
   7  public static SendGridMessage Run(string myQueueItem, ILogger log)
   8  {
   9      SendGridMessage message = new SendGridMessage()
  10      {
  11          Subject = "Order received on " + DateTime.Now.ToString()
  12      };
  13
  14      message.AddContent("text/plain", $"Hi there, we've received your order. We'll let you know agian when your order
  15
  16      return message;
  17  }
```

```
∨  Logs  Console                                          Reconnect  Copy logs  Pause  Clear  Expand
2019-01-26T11:20:39  Welcome, you are now connected to log-streaming service.
2019-01-26T11:20:46.028 [Information] Executing 'Functions.ServiceBusQueueTrigger1' (Reason='New ServiceBus message detected
on 'order'.', Id=7a2ef7c6-4305-4cf7-ba00-c3cd5780963d)
2019-01-26T11:20:46.103 [Information] Executed 'Functions.ServiceBusQueueTrigger1' (Succeeded, Id=7a2ef7c6-4305-4cf7-ba00-
c3cd5780963d)
```

Figure 2-24. *Testing the queue trigger function*

At the same time, you may receive an e-mail notification at the e-mail address you defined earlier, indicating that your order is being processed (see Figure 2-25).

Order received on 1/26/2019 11:19:50 AM   Inbox ×

via sendgrid.info   7:19 PM (3 minutes ago)
to me

Hi there, we've received your order. We'll let you know agian when your order is on its way. Order: 4 Unit of Surface Book 2

If you'd like to unsubscribe and stop receiving these emails click here.

↩ Reply   ➡ Forward

Figure 2-25. *E-mail sent from SendGrid output trigger*

Summary

In this chapter, you started by learning about the core Azure Functions programming model, and then you learned how to create a function from the quickstart or a template. You then moved on to several popular scenarios of Azure Functions including Webhook + API, timer-based functions, and finally the queue trigger functions.

CHAPTER 3

Accessing Data from Azure Functions

In the previous chapter, you learned about the programming model used in Azure Functions and saw a few popular templates. While most of the examples were done with C# Script directly in the Azure portal, in this chapter you will dive deeper into how to access Azure SQL Database in Azure Functions through Visual Studio 2019.

Overview of Azure SQL Database

Azure SQL Database (aka SQL Azure) is a platform-as-a-service (PaaS) relational database offered by Azure. The core engine of Azure SQL Database is based on SQL Server. The unique feature of the SQL database is that it is self-managed. In other words, the platform takes care of many tasks such as provisioning the server, installing the SQL Server software, setting up for high availability, and so much more. This allows developers to focus on building applications and allows database administrators (DBAs) to focus on tuning queries.

In 2018, Azure also released three similar managed databases, namely, Azure Database for MySQL, Azure Database for PostgreSQL, and Azure Database for MariaDB.

© Agus Kurniawan, Wely Lau 2019
A. Kurniawan and W. Lau, *Practical Azure Functions*,
https://doi.org/10.1007/978-1-4842-5067-9_3

Using Visual Studio 2019

Let's start by opening Visual Studio 2019. We encourage you to upgrade to the latest version if you haven't. You can do this by clicking the notification (flag) icon at the top right of Visual Studio 2019.

To start, select File ➤ New Project. Enter **function** in the search bar, and you will see the Azure Functions project template. Click Next and fill in the project name, location, and solution name, as shown in Figure 3-1. Click Create to proceed.

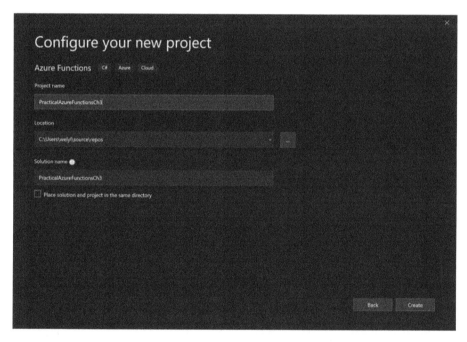

Figure 3-1. *Azure Functions template in Visual Studio*

You'll then be asked for the function version (use version 1 with the
.NET Framework or version 2 with .NET Standard/.NET Core). Let's
choose Azure Function v2 and select "Http trigger," as shown in Figure 3-2.
You can leave the options of Storage Account and "Access rights" at their
default values. Click OK.

Figure 3-2. *Http trigger in Visual Studio function template*

You will notice that Visual Studio generates some template code for
getting started (Figure 3-3). Click Run or press F5 to run it.

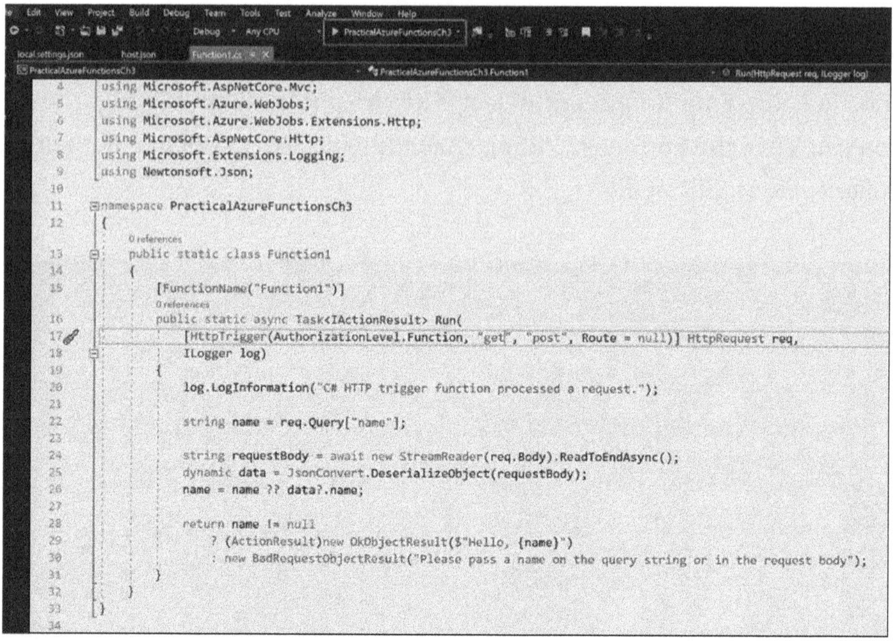

Figure 3-3. *Visual Studio–autogenerated code in Azure Functions*

You will notice that another console window shows up with some logs generated. Pay attention to the localhost URL, as highlighted in Figure 3-4.

```
 C:\Users\wellyl\AppData\Local\AzureFunctionsTools\Releases\2.17.0\cli\func.exe                                              —   □   ✕
[2/12/2019 11:24:53 AM]     "LockAcquisitionTimeout": "10675199.02:48:05.4775807",
[2/12/2019 11:24:53 AM]     "LockAcquisitionPollingInterval": "00:00:05",
[2/12/2019 11:24:53 AM]     "ListenerLockRecoveryPollingInterval": "00:01:00"
[2/12/2019 11:24:53 AM] }
[2/12/2019 11:24:53 AM] Starting JobHost
[2/12/2019 11:24:53 AM] Starting Host (HostId=minintpc20up7-903726221, InstanceId=14288306-7f1d-4d45-9fd4-93311f02e988,
Version=2.0.12285.0, ProcessId=37384, AppDomainId=1, InDebugMode=False, InDiagnosticMode=False, FunctionsExtensionVersio
n=)
[2/12/2019 11:24:53 AM] Loading functions metadata
[2/12/2019 11:24:53 AM] 1 functions loaded
[2/12/2019 11:24:53 AM] WorkerRuntime: dotnet. Will shutdown other standby channels
[2/12/2019 11:24:53 AM] Generating 1 job function(s)
[2/12/2019 11:24:53 AM] Found the following functions:
[2/12/2019 11:24:53 AM] PracticalAzureFunctionsCh3.Function1.Run
[2/12/2019 11:24:53 AM]
[2/12/2019 11:24:53 AM] Host initialized (420ms)
[2/12/2019 11:24:53 AM] Host started (434ms)
[2/12/2019 11:24:53 AM] Job host started
Hosting environment: Production
Content root path: C:\Users\wellyl\source\repos\PracticalAzureFunctions\PracticalAzureFunctionsCh3\bin\Debug\netcoreapp2.
1
Now listening on: http://0.0.0.0:7071
Application started. Press Ctrl+C to shut down.

Http Functions:

        Function1: [GET,POST] http://localhost:7071/api/Function1

[2/12/2019 11:24:59 AM] Host lock lease acquired by instance ID '000000000000000000000046439F9A'.
```

Figure 3-4. *Running an Azure Functions function locally*

Paste the URL into a browser and append **?name=Azure** at the end of the URL. If everything goes well, you should see "Hello, Azure" displayed in the browser.

As you can tell from the URL, your Azure Functions function now runs locally.

The following are the two main advantages of developing this locally over developing it directly on the cloud (through the Azure portal):

- With a powerful integrated development environment (IDE) like Visual Studio (or an editor like Visual Studio Code), the experience of authoring, testing, and debugging code is more convenient.

- When you work in an environment that does not have Internet access, you can continue writing your code and deploy it later when you have Internet access.

Coming back to the main topic of dealing with relational data in the SQL database, what you are going to do next is record every single HTTP request detail (such as message, client IP address, timestamp) to a SQL database table.

Creating Your SQL Database

Using Figure 3-5, create a SQL database on the Azure portal (`https://portal.azure.com`) by clicking the "+ Create a resource" button in the left menu; then choose Databases and SQL Database. Choose the appropriate subscription and resource group. Provide the database name as well. For the server, click "Create new" if you don't have an existing server.

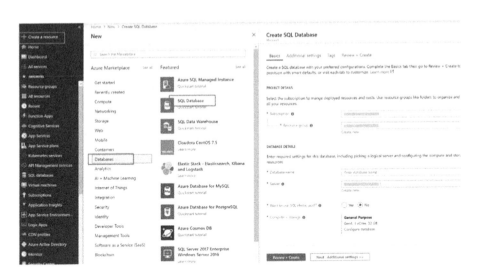

Figure 3-5. *Creating a SQL database*

The "New server" blade will appear (as shown in Figure 3-6). Fill in the details such as the server name, admin login, password, and location accordingly. Make sure you remember the username and password as you'll be using them in later steps.

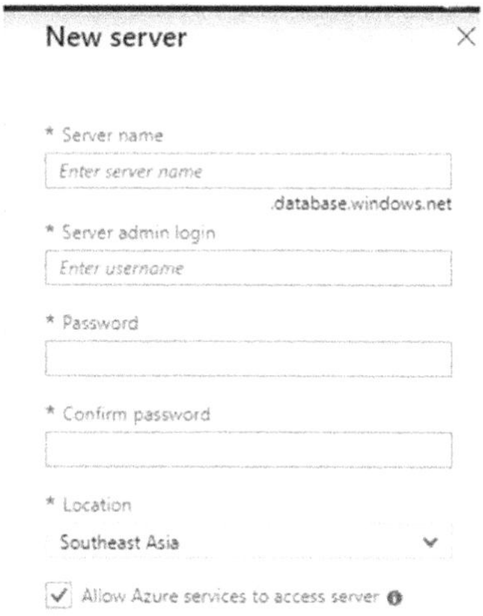

New server   ✕

* Server name

Enter server name

.database.windows.net

* Server admin login

Enter username

* Password

* Confirm password

* Location

Southeast Asia   ⌄

☑ Allow Azure services to access server ❶

Figure 3-6. *Creating the Azure SQL Database server*

The server in this context represents a virtual server, which you will connect to from your client app. You can also control the firewall to determine which IP addresses can connect to the server.

Coming back to the main "Create SQL Database" blade, you will see the "Elastic pool" option. An *elastic pool* in Azure SQL Database allows the user to create multiple databases while sharing a set number of resources at a set price. As you're not going to use this now, simply leave the "Elastic pool" option set to No, as shown in Figure 3-7.

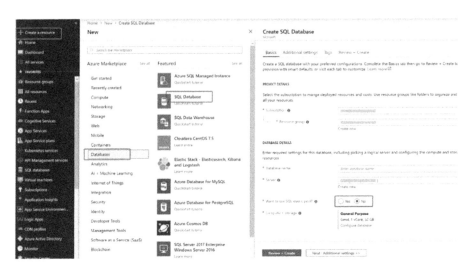

Figure 3-7. *Creating a SQL database*

For the "Compute + storage" option, choose "Configure database." Notice that another blade opens showing the details of the database configuration and size for various types of workloads such as Basic, Standard, and Premium. Each of the database's sizes is powered by a machine with a different set of configurations (vCPU, RAM, and IOPS). See Figure 3-8.

Figure 3-8. *Choosing the Azure SQL Database size*

Since this function is for demo purposes only, let's pick the most economical option by selecting Basic. You can increase the minimum database size from 100MB to 250GB. Click Apply. See Figure 3-9.

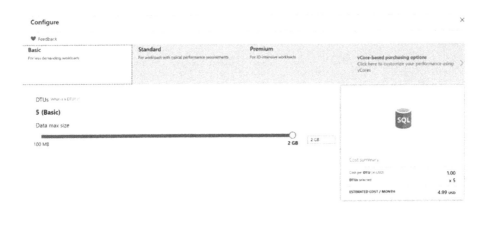

Figure 3-9. *Choosing the basic size*

Go back to the "Create SQL Database" blade again and click Review + Create and then Create to complete the creation process. It will take several minutes to create the database.

Once the database has been created, you will be able to explore and perform further configuration later.

Configuring a Firewall for a SQL Database Server

Another thing you need to do is to configure the firewall to allow access to a particular client IP address. The Client IP Firewall is a built-in feature in Azure SQL Database to enhance security, in addition to providing access with the username and password. Think about the scenario where your username and password are lost accidentally. With this feature, you still can restrict which IP address(es) can access your database.

To do that (as shown in Figure 3-10), click the server name of the Azure SQL server; then scroll in the left menu and click "Firewalls and virtual networks." Click the "+ Add client IP" option, and you'll notice that the rule name and the client IPs (starting and ending) will automatically be filled in. You can put the same value in the START IP and END IP fields, or you can enter a range.

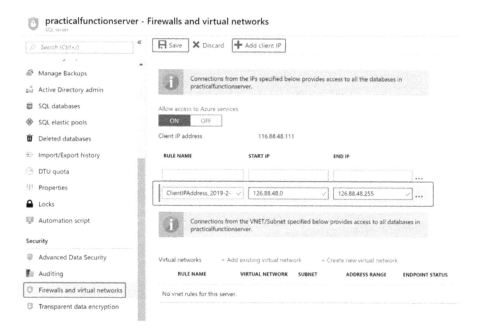

Figure 3-10. *Adding a client IP in the SQL Server firewall settings*

Connecting Azure SQL Database with SQL Server Management Studio

Since Azure SQL Database is a managed PaaS version of SQL Server, you can use the same tool that you use for the on-premise SQL Server, namely, SQL Server Management Studio.

You can download and install SQL Management Studio (SSMS) from `https://docs.microsoft.com/en-us/sql/ssms/download-sql-server-management-studio-ssms?view=sql-server-2017`. Currently, SSMS 17.9.1 is the latest General Availability (GA) version.

Before accessing Azure SQL Database from SSMS, you will need to take note of the connection string of Azure SQL Database in the Azure portal. To do that, click the "Connection strings" menu in the SQL Database blade, as shown as Figure 3-11. Depending on the type of your client app, you can choose ADO.NET, JDBC, ODBC, etc., accordingly. Notice that your username and password are not displayed because of security reasons.

Figure 3-11.   *Getting Azure SQL Database's connection string*

Upon the installation, click File ➤ Connect to object explorer.

1. Leave the "Server type" option set to Database Engine.

2. Enter the server name you created earlier (or you can get it from the connection string in Figure 3-12). The server name should end with the suffix `.database.windows.net`.

3. Choose SQL Server Authentication for the Authentication option.

4. Enter the login and password that you defined earlier.

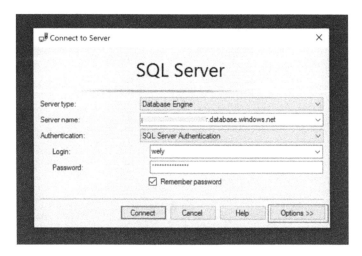

Figure 3-12. *Connecting to Azure SQL Database from SQL Server Management Studio*

The next step is to implicitly choose the database to which you want to connect. To do that, click the Options >> button and fill in the "Connect to database" field with the database name you defined earlier. Finally, click Connect. See Figure 3-13.

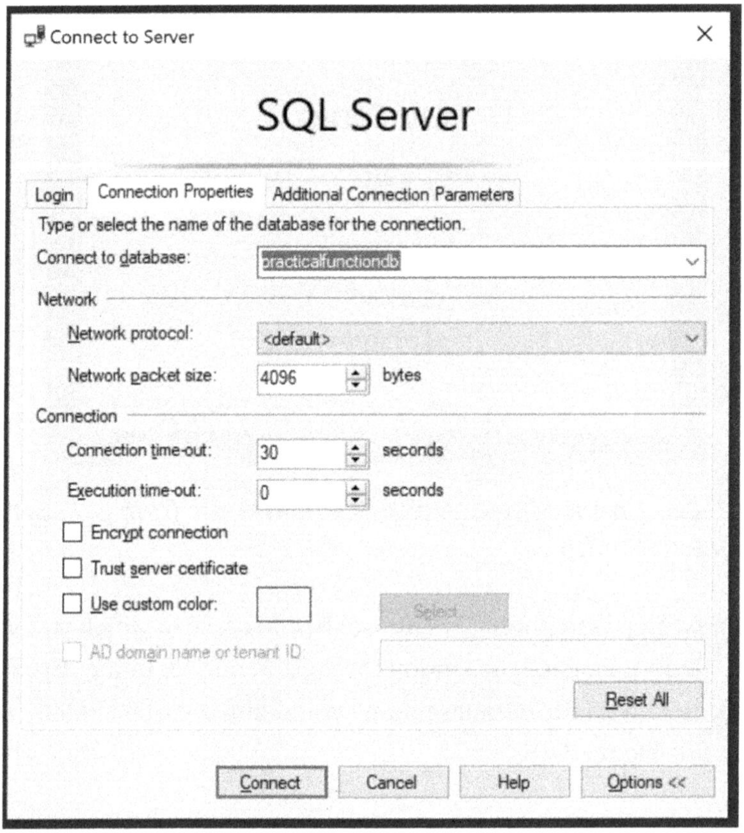

Figure 3-13. *Connection Properties tab*

If all the details are filled in correctly, you should be able to see the SQL database displayed in the Object Explorer, as shown in Figure 3-14.

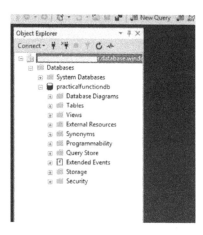

Figure 3-14. *Azure SQL Database and its objects in the Object Explorer*

If you encounter an error message indicating that your client IP address doesn't have access to the server, as shown in Figure 3-15, please revisit the "section 3.5" to configure the firewall correctly. Alternatively, you can click Sign In and add the firewall directly from SQL Server Management Studio.

Figure 3-15. *Adding a firewall rule from SQL Server Management Studio*

As you're planning to store every single request on the Azure function in a SQL database, you'll learn how to create a table now. To do that, expand the database you created earlier, right-click Tables, and choose New ➤ Table. See Figure 3-16.

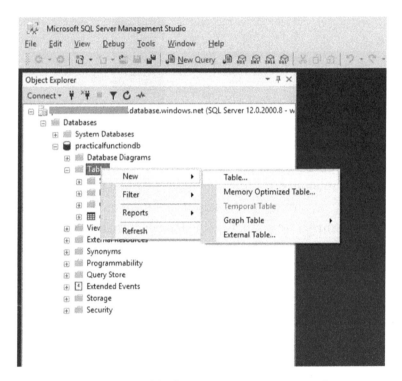

Figure 3-16. *Creating a table from Management Studio*

Define the table column with the details provided in Table 3-1.

Table 3-1. *Function Request Table*

Column Name	Data Type	Allow Nulls	Remarks
Id	Int	No	Set as the primary key. Set Identity specification to Yes (auto-increment). Leave Identity Increment and Seed set to 1.
ServerHost	Nvarchar(50)	No	This is to record the function's server host.
ClientIPAddress	Nvarchar(50)	No	This is to capture the client's IP address.
Message	Nvarchar(50)	No	The message produced upon entering the name parameter in the querystring.
DateTime	Datetime	No	

Save the table with a name of FunctionRequest.

You can also refer to the SQL Data Definition Language (DDL), as shown in Listing 3-1, if you prefer to create a table from script.

Listing 3-1. Data Definition Language to Create the FunctionRequest Table

```
CREATE TABLE [dbo].[FunctionRequest](
      [Id] [int] IDENTITY(1,1) NOT NULL,
      [ServerHost] [nvarchar](50) NOT NULL,
      [ClientIPAddress] [nvarchar](50) NOT NULL,
      [Message] [nvarchar](50) NOT NULL,
      [DateTime] [datetime] NOT NULL,
 CONSTRAINT [PK_FunctionRequest] PRIMARY KEY CLUSTERED
(
```

```
    [Id] ASC
)WITH (STATISTICS_NORECOMPUTE = OFF, IGNORE_DUP_KEY = OFF) ON
[PRIMARY]
) ON [PRIMARY]
GO
```

Configuring Azure Functions in Visual Studio

In this section, you'll let Azure Function's code interact with the SQL database you created earlier.

Accessing the SQL database from Azure Functions is similar to when using other project types such as ASP.NET Web/MVC, .NET Console, or even a Windows Forms app.

Make sure you provide the right connection string in the local settings, which eventually will be mapped to the application settings in the function app. To do that, let's go back to Visual Studio by right-clicking your project and clicking Publish. Then, click Edit Azure App Service Settings. As shown in Figure 3-17, once the Application Settings pop-up window appears, click + Add Setting and give the new app a name such as **sqldb_connection**; then click OK. Notice that there are two values (Local and Remote). This allows you to connect to a different database depending on where it's running. For example, it connects to the on-premise SQL Server as a local one, while it connects to Azure SQL Database instance when it's deployed to the cloud (remote).

Figure 3-17. *Application Settings pop-up in Visual Studio*

In this case, you can paste in the value for both Local and Remote from the Connection String menu (see the section 3.5). Make sure you've updated the username and password accordingly. Then click OK. The local value will be stored in the local.settings.json file, while the remote value will eventually be stored as an application setting in the function app.

Since you are using C# with .NET Core, you need to add the necessary libraries to access the SQL database, particularly in the System.Data. SqlClient assembly. To do that, right-click the project and then choose Manage NuGet Packages, as shown in Figure 3-18.

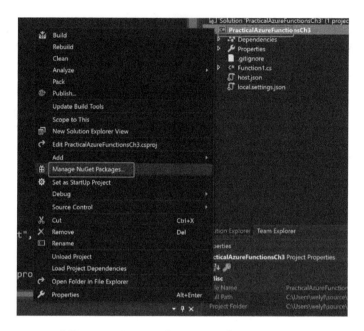

Figure 3-18. *Adding NuGet packages to the project*

Click the Browse menu, enter **System.Data.SqlClient**, and choose
the correct one, as shown in Figure 3-19. Change the version to the latest
stable version and click Install.

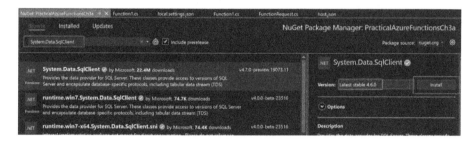

Figure 3-19. *Adding the SQLClient library from NuGet*

Click OK to preview the changes. Then click I Accept to accept the
license. You can verify whether the package was successfully installed by
clicking Dependencies ➤ Nuget under the project.

Writing Azure Functions Code in VS

You have done the necessary configuration on your Visual Studio project. The next step is to start coding.

You'll start by creating a class that represents the `FunctionRequest` table in the SQL database. To do that, right-click the project and choose Add ➤ New Item. Make sure that you've selected Visual C# in the left menu, choose Class, and then name the class `FunctionRequest.cs`. See Figure 3-20.

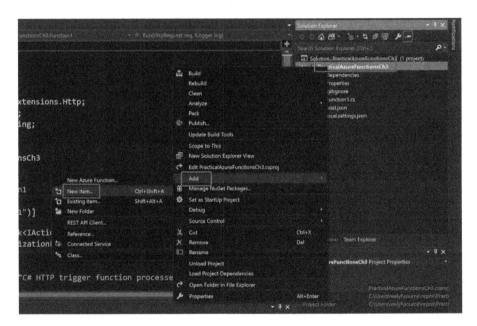

Figure 3-20. *Adding a new item in Visual Studio*

Add properties to the class, as shown in Listing 3-2.

Listing 3-2. Class for FunctionRequest

```
using System;

namespace PracticalAzureFunctionsCh3
{
    public class FunctionRequest
    {
        public int Id { get; set; }
        public string ServerHost { get; set; }
        public string ClientIPAddress { get; set; }
        public string Message { get; set; }
        public DateTime { get; set; }
    }
}
```

The next step is to update the function's code. By default, a function called Function1 was created when you created a function project in Visual Studio. Modify the code to what is shown in Listing 3-3.

Listing 3-3. Function's Main Code to Save to the Database

```
using System;
using System.IO;
using System.Threading.Tasks;
using Microsoft.AspNetCore.Mvc;
using Microsoft.Azure.WebJobs;
using Microsoft.Azure.WebJobs.Extensions.Http;
using Microsoft.AspNetCore.Http;
using Microsoft.Extensions.Logging;
using Newtonsoft.Json;
using System.Data.SqlClient;
```

```csharp
namespace PracticalAzureFunctionsCh3
{
    public static class Function1
    {
        [FunctionName("Function1")]
        public static async Task<IActionResult> Run(
            [HttpTrigger(AuthorizationLevel.Function, "get",
            "post", Route = null)] HttpRequest req, ILogger log)
        {
            log.LogInformation("C# HTTP trigger function
            processed a request.");

            string name = req.Query["name"];

            string requestBody = await new StreamReader(req.
            Body).ReadToEndAsync();
            dynamic data = JsonConvert.DeserializeObject(reques
            tBody);
            name = name ?? data?.name;

            FunctionRequest fr = new FunctionRequest();
            fr.ServerHost = req.Host.ToString();
            fr.ClientIPAddress = req.Headers["X-Forwarded-
            For"].ToString();
            fr.DateTime = DateTime.Now;
            fr.Message = "Hello " + name;

            if (name != null)
            {
                var str = Environment.
                GetEnvironmentVariable("sqldb_connection");
                try
                {
```

```csharp
using (SqlConnection conn = new
SqlConnection(str))
{
    conn.Open();
    var text = "INSERT INTO FunctionRequest
    (ClientIPAddress, ServerHost, Message,
    DateTime) VALUES (@clientipaddress,
    @serverhost, @message, @datetime)";

    using (SqlCommand cmd = new
    SqlCommand(text, conn))
    {
        cmd.Parameters.AddWithValue
        ("@clientipaddress",
        fr.ClientIPAddress);
        cmd.Parameters.AddWithValue
        ("@serverhost", fr.ServerHost);
        cmd.Parameters.AddWithValue
        ("@message", fr.Message);
        cmd.Parameters.AddWithValue
        ("@datetime", fr.DateTime);

        var rows = await cmd.
        ExecuteNonQueryAsync();
    }
}
return (ActionResult)new
OkObjectResult($"Message: \"{fr.Message}\"
from Your IP Address: {fr.ClientIPAddress}
has been recorded on {fr.DateTime.
ToString()}");
}
```

```
        catch (Exception ex)
        {
            return new BadRequestObjectResult("Some
            error occurs. Message : " + ex.Message);
        }
    }
    else
    {
        return new BadRequestObjectResult("Please pass
        a name on the query string or in the request
        body");
    }
        }
    }
}
```

In Listing 3-3, you first created the object fr from the FunctionRequest class and filled it with values from the function's HttpRequest. Subsequently, you retrieved the database connection string through Environment.GetEnvironmentVariable("sqldb_connection") and inserted the values into the database table. Finally, you displayed the message as a return value to the UI.

Running and Testing Azure Function Locally

You will build and run the Azure Functions function locally first before deploying it to the cloud. To do that, click Debug ➤ Start Debugging or simply press F5. Similar to what was covered earlier, now you'll copy the URL into the browser again and append ?name=LocalFunction. Then hit Enter.

Because you're running Visual Studio, you can put a breakpoint and debug over it. This will increase your development productivity tremendously.

If everything goes well, you should see a message like "Message: 'Hello LocalFunction' from Your IP Address: has been recorded on 2/19/2019 2:58:15 PM." You will notice that Client IP Address is empty. This is because HttpRequest's Headers["X-Forwarded-For"] doesn't apply when running locally. Verify your database table if you can find the new record that was just entered.

Deploying to Azure Functions

Once you'll all set locally, the next step is to deploy the function to the cloud and to verify whether it works as expected. To do that, go back to Visual Studio, right-click your project, and click Publish. You can either choose to deploy to a newly created function app or select an existing one (see Figure 3-21).

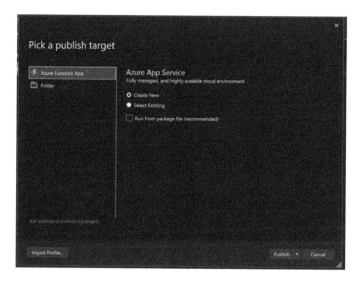

Figure 3-21. *Publishing to Azure Functions from Visual Studio*

In our case, we like to deploy to a new one; as such, choose the Create New option and click Publish.

You will need to authenticate with your Azure credentials from Visual Studio if you haven't done so. As shown in Figure 3-22, the subscription will show accordingly, and you can decide if you'd like to create this new function app as part of an existing resource group or to create it in a new resource group. Similarly, this applies to the hosting plan as well as the storage account. Then click Create.

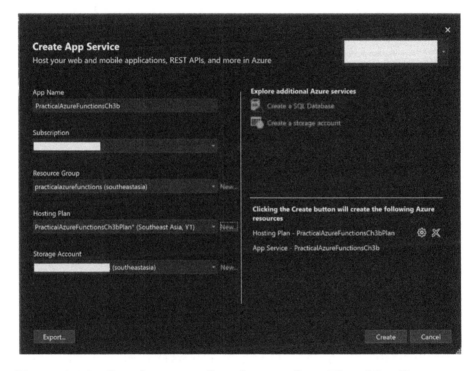

Figure 3-22. *Creating a new function app from Visual Studio*

It will take a few moments to validate and deploy.

You may encounter the dialog box shown in Figure 3-23. This happens because the default version of Azure Functions in Azure Cloud is 1.0 (.NET Framework) if you chose 2.0 (.NET Core) during the project creation in Visual Studio. Choosing Yes will allow Visual Studio to update the version of Azure Functions in Azure Cloud to 2.0 (.NET Core).

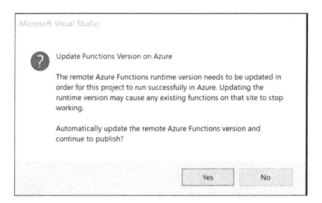

Figure 3-23. Updating the Azure Functions version

Running and Testing Function Apps in the Cloud

Once the deployment has been successfully completed, navigate to the Azure portal and browse your function apps.

Before running the application, let's examine if the application setting for the SQL database's connection string has been successfully stored. To do that, navigate to your function app's Overview tab. Click the "Application settings" link. Then scroll further down until you discover the "Application settings" section, as shown as Figure 3-24. You can also click it to verify whether the value has been entered correctly.

Figure 3-24. *Azure Functions application settings*

Let's test if the function can be run properly. Like what you did earlier, perform the same steps, except use the Azure Functions public URL.

If it goes well, you should see a message such as "Message: 'Hello Azure Functions' from Your IP Address: 111.222.111.222:12345 has been recorded on 2/24/2019 10:59:57 AM." You can also verify if a new record has been saved to your database table.

Summary

You started this chapter by getting an overview of Azure SQL Database, the PaaS relational database service in Azure. You then created and configured an Azure SQL Database instance in Azure. Subsequently, you used Visual Studio 2019 as an IDE to write the code that interacts with the SQL database. Finally, you tested on the local machine as well as on Azure Cloud.

You'll learn about NoSQL and Azure Functions in the upcoming chapter.

CHAPTER 4

Accessing Cosmos DB in Azure Functions

NoSQL databases have been extremely popular in recent years. In this chapter, you will learn how to access Cosmos DB, the primary NoSQL database in Azure Functions.

Introduction to NoSQL Databases and Azure Cosmos DB

The term *NoSQL* refers to database systems that store data in a wider variety of data models than relational databases such as documents, key-value pairs, or graphs. This is a different concept than the conventional relational database management system (RDBMS) used in the SQL Server, Oracle, and MySQL databases that have been around for decades.

Though it's not mandatory, NoSQL databases are often deployed in distributed nodes across multiple partitions rather than in single-instance deployments.

There are several major reasons why NoSQL has gotten more popular in recent years including scalability, performance, and flexibility. Unlike an RDBMS, which typically scales vertically (by adding hardware such as CPU or memory) to the server, NoSQL scales horizontally across multiple servers.

© Agus Kurniawan, Wely Lau 2019
A. Kurniawan and W. Lau, *Practical Azure Functions*,
https://doi.org/10.1007/978-1-4842-5067-9_4

Azure Cosmos DB is an evolution of a document-based database engine known as Azure Document DB. Several attributes make Azure Cosmos DB a unique NoSQL database.

- **Multimodel and multi-API:** Azure Cosmos DB provides different models and APIs including SQL (core), MongoDB, Cassandra, Azure Tables, and Gremlin (Graph). This means an application can access a Cosmos DB just like accessing another MongoDB database with the same connection string format, as shown in Figure 4-1.

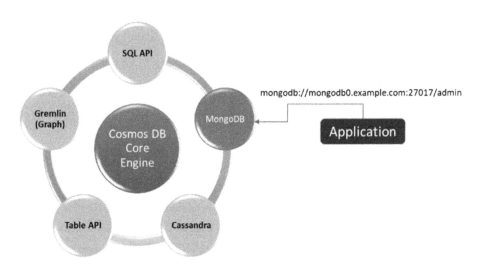

Figure 4-1. *Multi-API in Azure Cosmos DB*

- **Globally distributed:** You can deploy the Cosmos DB databases across the globe easily with just a few clicks in the Azure portal, as shown in Figure 4-2, or a few commands through the command line.

Figure 4-2. *Globally distributed NoSQL database*

- **Throughput, consistency, and latency SLA in addition to an availability SLA:** Most of the database services on the market today offer an availability SLA. However, Azure Cosmos DB provides a more comprehensive SLA that includes provisions for throughput, consistency, and latency. At the time this book was written, the service offers 99.99 percent guarantees for availability, throughput, latency, and consistency. Refer to the latest SLA at `https://azure. microsoft.com/en-in/support/legal/sla/cosmos-db`.

Provisioning an Azure Cosmos DB Account

We'll get right into the action by creating an Azure Cosmos DB database in this section. To do that, go to the Azure portal, and click the "+ Create a resource" button. Once the blade is opens, choose Databases and scroll down to locate Azure Cosmos DB, as shown in Figure 4-3.

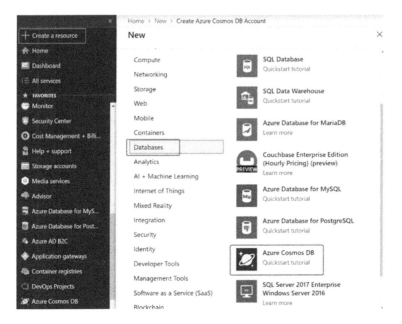

Figure 4-3. *Locating Azure Cosmos DB in the Azure portal*

As an alternative, you can also type **Cosmos** in the Search the Marketplace box to find Azure Cosmos DB.

Click Azure Cosmos DB, and you'll immediately see another blade called Create Azure Cosmos DB Account appear. Like the other resource creation experiences, fill in the details (such as Subscription, Resource Group, Location, and Account Name) accordingly.

One important field here is for the Cosmos DB API, as shown in Figure 4-4. This will enable the core engine of Cosmos DB to behave like the API you choose. For example, once you choose the MongoDB API and have your application connect to Cosmos DB, your app will just treat that Cosmos DB database like a typical MongoDB database. Note that once you've chosen the API during creation, you won't be able to change it.

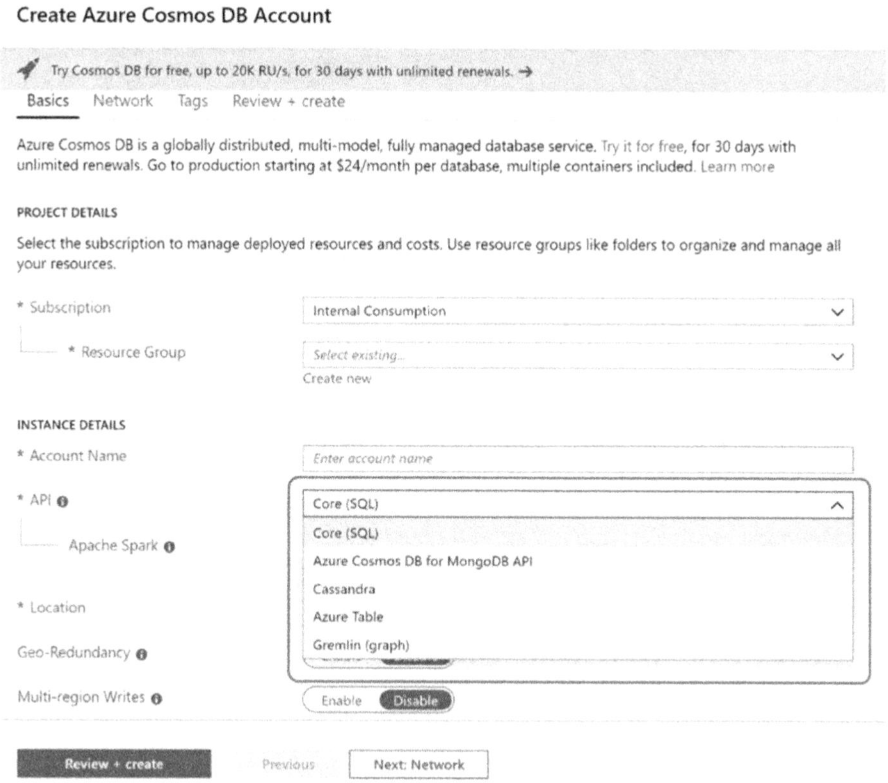

Create Azure Cosmos DB Account

🚀 Try Cosmos DB for free, up to 20K RU/s, for 30 days with unlimited renewals. →

Basics   Network   Tags   Review + create

Azure Cosmos DB is a globally distributed, multi-model, fully managed database service. Try it for free, for 30 days with unlimited renewals. Go to production starting at $24/month per database, multiple containers included. Learn more

PROJECT DETAILS

Select the subscription to manage deployed resources and costs. Use resource groups like folders to organize and manage all your resources.

* Subscription	Internal Consumption ∨
* Resource Group	Select existing... ∨
	Create new

INSTANCE DETAILS

* Account Name	Enter account name
* API ⓘ	Core (SQL) ∧
	Core (SQL)
Apache Spark ⓘ	Azure Cosmos DB for MongoDB API
	Cassandra
* Location	Azure Table
	Gremlin (graph)
Geo-Redundancy ⓘ	
Multi-region Writes ⓘ	Enable Disable

Review + create   Previous   Next: Network

Figure 4-4. *Creating a Cosmos DB account*

In this example, let's choose Core (SQL).

Another field that you need to look at is Geo-Redundancy. Enabling this field will provision another database instance in the paired region based on your selection of the (primary) Location field. As an example, when you pick (Asia Pacific) Southeast Asia as the primary location, " Asia will be automatically selected as the secondary region. You can see the paired region by clicking the "i" icon next to the Geo-Redundancy field, as shown in Figure 4-5. Alternatively, you can check out the complete list of Azure paired regions at https://docs.microsoft.com/en-us/azure/best-practices-availability-paired-regions.

Figure 4-5. *Geo-Redundancy field in Cosmos DB settings*

In this case, let's just leave the setting as Disable since you can turn it on later.

The next field is Multi-region Writes, which is also a powerful capability of Cosmos DB. This capability enables you to provision multiple databases across different regions with readable and writable access. You can leave it as Disable in this case, as shown in Figure 4-6.

Figure 4-6. *Multi-region Writes option*

There are two optional steps: Network and Tags. As you are not going to use both in this example, you can go ahead and click "Review + create." It will take a few minutes to provision the Cosmos DB account.

Once the account has been successfully provisioned, you will be able to access the Cosmos DB Overview page, which shows the accessible URI address, write and read locations, and the list of collections, as shown in Figure 4-7.

Figure 4-7. *Cosmos DB Overview page*

Dealing with Databases, Containers, and Items

You then need to create a database in this Cosmos DB account. To do that, click Data Explorer in the left menu. We'll show how to create a new container along with a database in this section. To do that, click New Container. Fill in the following details:

- Set the database ID to **IceCreamDB**. The database basically serves as the unit of management of the respective objects.

- Set the container ID to **Rating**. A container is analogous to a collection (in the MongoDB API) or a table (in the Cassandra API or Table API).

- Set the storage capacity to **Unlimited**.

- Set the partition key to `/ProductId`. This is like the concept of a shared key, which is used to spread the incoming data across multiple partitions. You can learn more about choosing the appropriate partition key at `https://docs.microsoft.com/en-us/azure/cosmos-db/partitioning-overview#choose-partitionkey`.

- Set Throughput to **400**, which is the minimum throughput you can define. The throughput (either at the database or container level) will impact the price.

- Leave the other fields at their defaults.

As illustrated in Figure 4-8, you can click OK to proceed.

You might notice that there is a terminology difference depending on the API that you chose during provisioning time. For more details about the terminology, you can visit `https://docs.microsoft.com/en-us/azure/cosmos-db/databases-containers-items`.

Figure 4-8. *Creating a new container in Cosmos DB*

Cosmos DB Trigger in Azure Functions

The next step is to create a Visual Studio project with a Cosmos DB trigger for Azure Functions. At the time this book was written, the Cosmos DB trigger in Azure Functions supports only the Core (SQL) API. This also applies to bindings, which will be discussed in the following section.

In this section, we'll show how to create an Azure Functions function that listens to the Rating container for any new item. If the rating is lower than 3, it will enqueue a message into the lowratings queue residing in Azure Queue storage.

To perform this task, create a new Visual Studio project by choosing an Azure Functions template and giving the project a name like **PracticalAzureFunctionCh4**, similar to what you did in Chapter 3.

As shown in Figure 4-9, you can then choose Cosmos DB Trigger from the trigger template list. For the storage account, change the drop-down from Storage Emulator to Browse to select your preferred storage account. Subsequently fill in the "Connection string setting" field with a connection string label such as **icecreamdbcs**. Note that it will be the label of the connection string; you will fill in the connection string's actual value in the JSON file later. Next, fill in the "Database name" and "Collection name" fields, respectively, with the values you specified earlier in the section 4.4. Finally, click OK to complete the project creation.

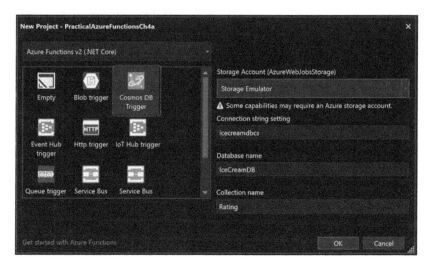

Figure 4-9. *Azure Functions template fields*

The next step is to add `Microsoft.Azure.WebJobs.Extensions.`
`Storage` through NuGet. As such, perform the same actions as you did in
the section 4.4. You can verify whether the package has been successfully
by going to the Installed tab, as shown in Figure 4-10.

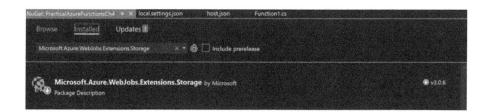

Figure 4-10. *Verifying the WebJobs.Extensions.Storage NuGet*
package

Navigate to `Function1.cs`, which is generated automatically by Visual
Studio. Replace the code in the namespace scope with the code snippet
shown in Listing 4-1.

Listing 4-1. Function's Main Code for Cosmos DB Trigger with Queue Return

```
public static class Function1
{
    [FunctionName("Function1")]
    [return: Queue("lowratings")]
    public static string Run([CosmosDBTrigger(
        databaseName: "IceCreamDB",
        collectionName: "Rating",
        ConnectionStringSetting = "icecreamdbcs",
        LeaseCollectionName = "leases",
        CreateLeaseCollectionIfNotExists = true)]
        IReadOnlyList<Document> input, ILogger log)
    {
        if (input != null && input.Count > 0)
        {
            log.LogInformation("Documents modified " +
            input.Count);
            log.LogInformation("First document Id " +
            input[0].Id);
            if (input[0].GetPropertyValue<int>("Rating") < 3)
            {
                string ratingAndReview = input[0].ToString();
                return ratingAndReview;
            }
            return null;
        }
        else return null;
    }
}
```

As defined, the function will run when any changes are made to the Rating container in the IceCreamDB database.

Notice that we have made several changes to the template's code, as listed here:

- We added the [return: Queue("lowratings")] attribute to the Run() method. This tells the Azure Functions function to return a message to the lowratings queue.

- We added the CreateLeaseCollectionIfNotExists = true attribute to the input parameter. As you can tell from the name, this will basically create a lease collection (or container) to the database if it doesn't exist. A lease collection is a special collection in Cosmos DB that is used to track the change feed reading progress per partition.

- Within the Run() method's body, you basically try to return a queue message consisting of [rating] [review] if the rating is less than 3.

The last thing you need to do before running the code locally is to navigate to the local.settings.json file. This is the file where you map the label (also known as the *key*) to the actual value. The value of AzureWebJobsStorage was filled in during the section 4.4. You now need to add the Cosmos DB connection string. Fill in the connection string label with **icecreamdbcs** (unless you used a different label). To get the actual value of the connection string, navigate to the Azure portal, choose Azure Cosmos DB, and click the Keys menu. Copy the value of the Primary Connection String field, as indicated in Figure 4-11.

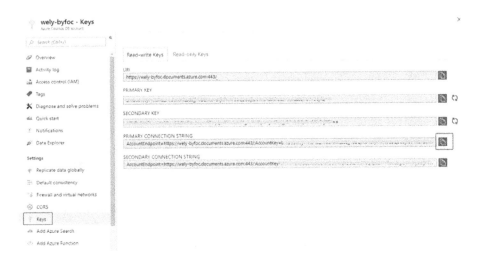

Figure 4-11. *Cosmos DB connection string*

Then paste it as the `icecreamdbcs` value in the `local.settings.json` file in Visual Studio. Your `local.settings.json` file should look like Figure 4-12.

```
{
    "IsEncrypted": false,
    "Values": {
        "AzureWebJobsStorage":
        "DefaultEndpointsProtocol=https;AccountName=practicalazurefun
                                     ;EndpointSuffix=core.windows.net",
        "FUNCTIONS_WORKER_RUNTIME": "dotnet",
        "icecreamdbcs": "AccountEndpoint=https://wely-
        byfoc.documents.azure.com:443/;AccountKey=
                  ;"
    }
}
```

Figure 4-12. *local.settings.json file*

Let's run the function locally by pressing F5 in Visual Studio. If all goes well, you should see the function host running locally in another console, as shown in Figure 4-13.

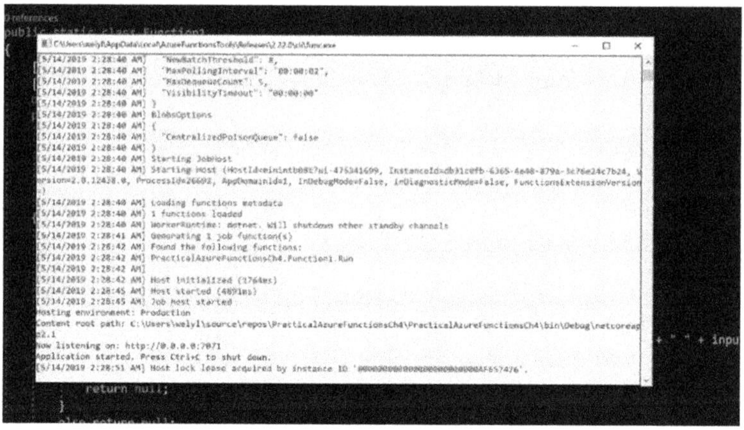

Figure 4-13. *Azure Functions function running locally*

Since the trigger of this function reacts to any changes on the Rating container in IceCreamDB, you'll want to put a breakpoint in the Azure Functions function's code if you'd like to see how it is being triggered. To do that, navigate to the first line of the function's code and hit F9 on the keyboard or choose Debug ➤ Toggle Breakpoint in Visual Studio. You should see the breakpoint with a red dot set, as illustrated in Figure 4-14.

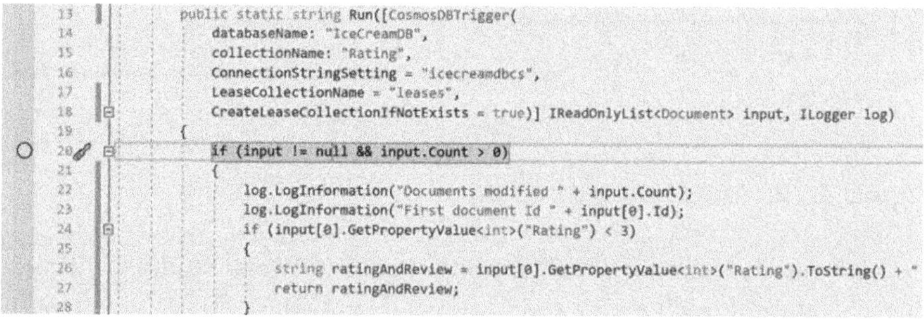

Figure 4-14. *Toggling the breakpoint in Azure Functions code in Visual Studio*

You can now add a new item to the Rating container. To do that, navigate back to your Azure portal, click Data Explorer, and then expand IceCreamDB, Rating, and Items. Click New Item, as shown in Figure 4-15.

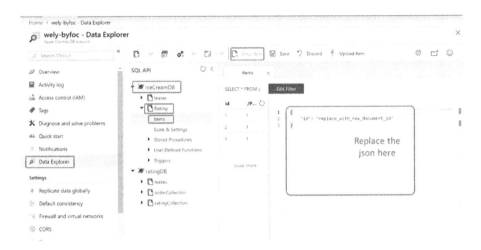

Figure 4-15. *Inserting a new item in Cosmos DB through the Data Explorer*

Subsequently, replace the JSON content with the code in Listing 4-2.

Listing 4-2. New Item in JSON Format

```
{
  "id" : "1",
  "ProductId" : "1",
  "Username" : "yourname",
  "Rating" : 2,
  "Review" : "I am disappointed with the Vanilla flavor"
}
```

Click Save, and if the save is successful, you will notice that the additional JSON elements (such as _rid, _self, _etag, etc.) have been added automatically, as shown in Figure 4-16.

Figure 4-16. *The item has been successfully saved.*

If you have done the configuration properly, Visual Studio will immediately stop at the breakpoint you set earlier with the yellow color background, as shown in Figure 4-17.

```
18         CreateLeaseCollectionIfNotExists = true)] IReadOnlyList<Document> input, ILogger log
19       {
20         if (input != null && input.Count > 0)
21         {
22             log.LogInformation("Documents modified " + input.Count);
23             log.LogInformation("First document Id " + input[0].Id);
24             if (input[0].GetPropertyValue<int>("Rating") < 3)
25             {
26                 string ratingAndReview = input[0].GetPropertyValue<int>("Rating").ToString()
```

Figure 4-17. *Debugging in Azure Functions*

You then can navigate by Step Into or Step Over or Continue just like how you typically perform a debugging session. If you press F5 or click Continue, the code will run and check whether the rating is less than 3. Since the value of the rating in the JSON file shown in Listing 4-2 is 2, the function should return the item in JSON format as a message to the Azure Storage queue named lowratings.

You can verify this by navigating to your Storage account in the Azure portal and then choosing the `lowratings` queue, as shown in Figure 4-18.

Figure 4-18. *Verifying messages in the queue storage*

Cosmos DB Bindings in Azure Functions

Conceptually, input and output bindings are similar to the Azure Storage blob bindings discussed in Chapter 2.

In this section, we'll show you how to follow up on the `lowratings` message. Imagine the use case where customer service reaches out to a customer to get more detailed feedback about why a given rating is low in order to improve the product. The details of the feedback and follow-up action will be eventually stored in another container in Cosmos DB through Azure Functions' Cosmos DB output bindings.

Start by creating another container named **FeedbackAndAction** with `/Username` as the partition key in Data Explorer in the Azure portal, as shown in Figure 4-19.

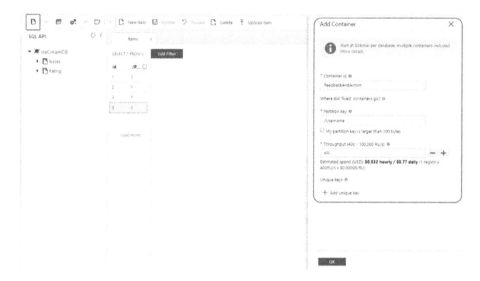

Figure 4-19. *Adding a FeedbackAndAction container in Cosmos DB*

Then click OK to complete the creation process.

Let's switch to Visual Studio as you'll be creating another Azure Functions function that will be listening to the lowratings queue and saving the data into the FeedbackAndAction container. To do that, right-click the Visual Studio project and then choose Add ➤ New Azure Function. Name the function **FollowupFunction**, as shown in Figure 4-20.

Figure 4-20. *Adding a follow-up function*

The next step is to add a JSON library named `Newtonsoft.Json` in the NuGet package manager, as shown in Figure 4-21.

Figure 4-21. *Adding the Newtonsoft.json package from NuGet*

Go back to the `FollowupFunction.cs` file in Visual Studio and replace all the code within the namespace with the code in Listing 4-3.

Listing 4-3. Follow-up Function's Code

```
public static class FollowupFunction
    {
        [FunctionName("FollowupFunction")]
        public static void Run([QueueTrigger("lowratings",
        Connection = "AzureWebJobsStorage")]string myQueueItem,
            [CosmosDB(databaseName: "IceCreamDB",
            collectionName: "FeedbackAndAction",
            ConnectionStringSetting = "icecreamdbcs")]out
            dynamic document,
            ILogger log)
        {
            log.LogInformation($"C# Queue trigger function
            processed: {myQueueItem}");

            dynamic obj = JValue.Parse(myQueueItem);
            document = new FeedbackAndAction()
            {
                Id = obj.id.ToString(),
                ProductId = obj.ProductId.ToString(),
                Username = obj.Username.ToString(),
                DetailFeedback = "The customer finds the ice
                cream is too sweet",
                NextAction = "Inform the kitchen to reduce the
                sugar"
            };
        }
    }
```

Several changes are made, as follows:

- We inserted a document with Cosmos DB properties such as databaseName, collectionName, and ConnectionStringSetting for the second parameter in the Run() method. This basically tells Azure Functions to perform an output binding with the document.

- Within the Run() method, you use JValue to parse the queue message, which is in JSON format. Subsequently, you fill in the document parameters with the respective values.

Let's run the function by hitting F5 in Visual Studio. If there isn't any message in the lowratings queue, you can add a new item in the Rating container or update an existing item. Make sure to change the Rating property to value less than 3.

You can verify whether the function ran successfully by checking out the Items menu in the FeedbackAndAction container, as shown in Figure 4-22.

Figure 4-22. *Verifying the FeedbackAndAction container*

Summary

You started this chapter by learning about the concept of NoSQL databases. Then we discussed the capabilities of Cosmos DB. We then covered how to provision a Cosmos DB account, database, and container. Finally, you learned how Cosmos DB triggers and bindings work.

CHAPTER 5

Web Back-End System

In this chapter, you'll explore how Azure Functions can make interacting with a web application more productive. You'll also build a simple project to see how web applications and Azure Functions can work together.

The following topics will be covered:

- Introduction to Azure Functions for web applications
- How to develop a web application with Azure Functions
- How to deploy Azure Functions to Microsoft Azure

Introduction to Azure Functions for Web Applications

There are many web application platforms that you can use to implement your web application. ASP.NET, PHP, JSP, and Node.js are just a few examples of web application platforms that web developers can choose. Each web platform provides specific features for implementing a web system.

In general, a web application has a database to store its data and session, as described in Figure 5-1. A web application can be hosted on a public host. You also can publish a web application to a cloud server such as Azure, AWS, or Google Cloud.

© Agus Kurniawan, Wely Lau 2019
A. Kurniawan and W. Lau, *Practical Azure Functions*,
https://doi.org/10.1007/978-1-4842-5067-9_5

To develop a web application, developers usually use a web framework from a web platform. You also need a web server to run a web application. Using an integrated development tool (IDE) is one way to accelerate your development.

Azure Functions provides some models to enable you to work with web applications. Technically, from a security perspective, a web application usually accepts the HTTP protocol, so one of the ways to connect Azure Functions to a web application is to use the HTTP protocol.

In this chapter, you'll use Azure Functions with an HTTP trigger to interact with a web application.

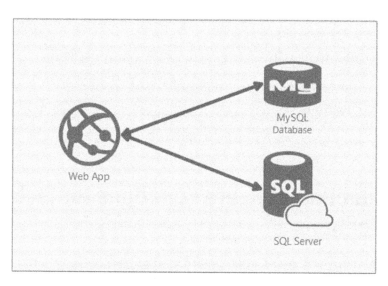

Figure 5-1. *A general web application*

Building a To-Do Web Application

In this section, you'll see how to build a simple web application that accesses Azure Functions. The application will be a to-do web application. You can add tasks to the web application. Furthermore, the web application calls Azure Functions to store the tasks in a database.

In general, you can implement the demo as shown in Figure 5-2. You will build a web app in Azure Functions by applying an HTTP trigger. This scenario will provide services so you can store the task data into the SQL database. Azure Functions also can serve up task data to the public.

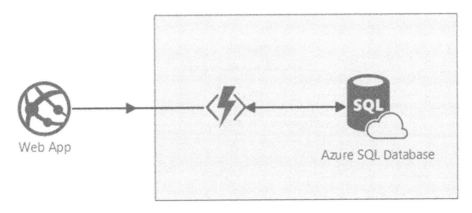

Figure 5-2. *Azure Functions and web applications*

For the implementation, you can use an ASP.NET Core web application. This application will consume Azure Functions to store and retrieve data from Azure SQL Database. You will need an active Azure account to deploy your project to Microsoft Azure.

In the following section, you'll create a project for Azure SQL Database.

Creating an Azure SQL Database Instance

You can use Azure SQL Database as the data back end. You can use an existing Azure SQL Database instance or create a new one. You can perform this task with the Azure portal at https://portal.azure.com. Figure 5-3 shows a new database being created named **azurefuncdb**.

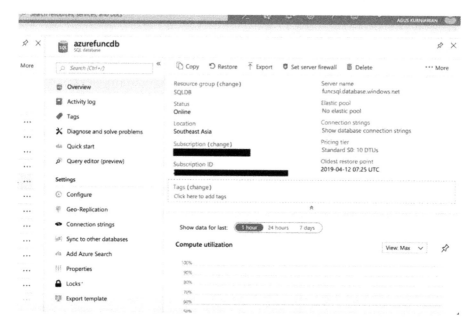

Figure 5-3. *New Azure SQL Database instance*

Next, you can create a table to store tasks using the web query editor. Execute the following SQL scripts to create the Todo table:

```
CREATE TABLE [dbo].[Todo](
      [id] [int] IDENTITY(1,1) NOT NULL,
      [todo] [varchar](50) NOT NULL,
      [posted] [datetime] NOT NULL,
 CONSTRAINT [PK_Todo] PRIMARY KEY CLUSTERED
(
      [id] ASC
)WITH (PAD_INDEX = OFF, STATISTICS_NORECOMPUTE = OFF, IGNORE_
DUP_KEY = OFF, ALLOW_ROW_LOCKS = ON, ALLOW_PAGE_LOCKS = ON) ON
[PRIMARY]
) ON [PRIMARY]
GO
```

To connect the web application to the Azure SQL Database instance, you need a database connection string. You can get this setting in the "Connection strings" menu from your database in Azure SQL Database. Copy the ADO.NET connection string data as shown in Figure 5-4.

Figure 5-4. *Database connection string*

You should change the {your_username} and {your_password} values for your Azure SQL Database configuration.

Next, you'll create a project for Azure Functions.

Creating an Azure Functions Project

You created a project for Azure Functions in the previous chapter. For this demo, you can create an Azure Functions project with C# as the programming language, as shown in Figure 5-5.

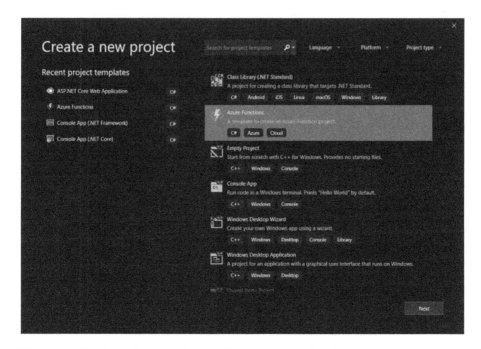

Figure 5-5. *Creating an Azure Functions project*

For the example implementation, create an Azure Functions project called **TodoFunctions**. You can use the "HTTP trigger" project template, as shown in Figure 5-6. After creating a project, you can continue to develop the Azure Functions program.

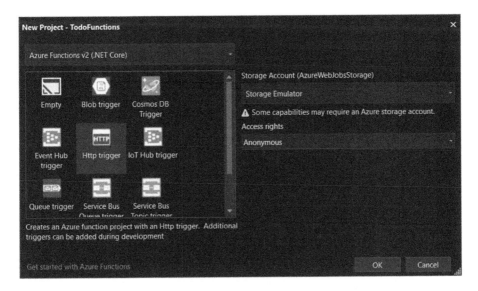

Figure 5-6. *HTTP trigger project template for Azure Functions*

Developing an Azure Functions Program

In this section, you'll develop a program for Azure Functions. The program will store and retrieve tasks from your Azure SQL Database instance. Figure 5-7 shows the general project structure, which consists of three files.

- The Todo.cs file is a model object for tasks.

- The AzureSQLDB.cs file is a data access object to perform SQL queries against Azure SQL Database.

- The ToDoFunc.cs file is an Azure Functions implementation.

You will implement these files in this section.

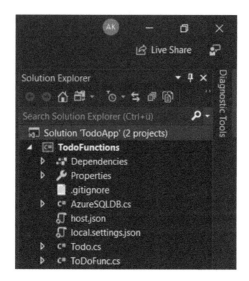

Figure 5-7. *Project structure for TodoFunctions*

First, you'll create a model for tasks. Create a class called Todo and define three properties for the Todo model: Id, TodoMessage, and Posted. You can write this code:

```
using System;

namespace TodoFunctions
{
    public class Todo
    {
        public int Id { get; set; }
        public string TodoMessage { get; set; }
        public DateTime Posted { get; set; }
    }
}
```

Next, create a data access object to interact with Azure SQL Database. You can create a class called AzureSQLDB and define two static methods, GetAllTodo() and InsertTodo(). The GetAllTodo() method is used to retrieve all tasks from Azure SQL Database. The InsertTodo() method is used to insert a task into the Azure SQL Database instance.

To access the Azure SQL Database instance, you can use ADO.NET from the SqlClient package. You define the System.Data.SqlClient package in the AzureSQLDB object, like so:

```
using System.Data.SqlClient;
```

In the GetAllTodo() method, you get a database connection string by calling the Environment.GetEnvironmentVariable() method. You define azure_sql for the database connection string name. You can also define a list variable as a collection of Todo objects.

```
public static List<Todo> GetAllTodo()
{
    List<Todo> list = new List<Todo>();
    string db = Environment.GetEnvironmentVariable("azure_sql");
```

You can use a SqlConnection object to open a connection to Azure SQL Database with a certain database connection string. You pass a SQL query to the SqlCommand object to retrieve all the tasks from the Todo table.

All the tasks are stored in a collection of Todo objects using the SqlDataReader object. The following is the implementation code:

```
    try
    {
        using (SqlConnection conn = new SqlConnection(db))
        {
            conn.Open();
            var text = "SELECT * from [Todo]";
```

```
        using (SqlCommand cmd = new SqlCommand(text, conn))
        {
            var rd = cmd.ExecuteReader();
            while (rd.Read())
            {
                var o = new Todo();
                o.Id = (int)rd["id"];
                o.TodoMessage = (string)rd["todo"];
                o.Posted = (DateTime)rd["posted"];

                list.Add(o);

            }
            rd.Close();
        }
    }
}
catch (Exception)
{
}
```

Next, you declare the InsertTodo() method to insert a task into Azure SQL Database. This method needs a task name as the method input. First, you get a database connection string from the azure_sql setting.

```
public static bool InsertTodo(string todo)
{
    string db = Environment.GetEnvironmentVariable("azure_sql");
```

You can use the SQL query to insert data into Azure SQL Database. You can perform this step using the SqlCommand object. You call ExecuteNonQuery() from the SqlCommand object to insert data into the database.

```
using (SqlConnection conn = new SqlConnection(db))
{
    conn.Open();
    var text = "INSERT INTO [Todo](todo,posted) VALUES
    (@todo,getdate())";

    using (SqlCommand cmd = new SqlCommand(text, conn))
    {
        cmd.Parameters.Add(new SqlParameter("@todo", todo));
        cmd.ExecuteNonQuery();

    }
}
```

Last, you need to edit the Azure Functions code in the TodoFunc.cs file. First, declare all required packages for your project, as shown here:

```
using System.Threading.Tasks;
using Microsoft.AspNetCore.Mvc;
using Microsoft.Azure.WebJobs;
using Microsoft.Azure.WebJobs.Extensions.Http;
using Microsoft.AspNetCore.Http;
using Microsoft.Extensions.Logging;
using Newtonsoft.Json;
using System.Data.SqlClient;
```

When you create a project for Azure Functions with an HTTP trigger, you will get a sample program. You can modify this code for your project scenario. For example, you can define the Azure Functions function with the name ToDoFunc so you can handle HTTP GET and HTTP POST requests from clients.

If you receive an HTTP GET request, you perform a SQL query to retrieve all the tasks from the database. You call the GetAllTodo() method from the AzureSQLDB object.

```
public static class ToDoFunc
{
    [FunctionName("ToDoFunc")]
    public static async Task<IActionResult> Run(
        [HttpTrigger(AuthorizationLevel.Anonymous, "get",
        "post", Route = null)] HttpRequest req,
        ILogger log)
    {
        log.LogInformation("TODO HTTP trigger function
        processed a request.");

        if(req.Method.ToLower() == "get")
        {
            var list = AzureSQLDB.GetAllTodo();

            return (ActionResult)new
            OkObjectResult(JsonConvert.SerializeObject(list));
        }
```

Furthermore, if you receive an HTTP POST request, you perform a SQL query to insert a task into the database. You parse the incoming JSON data from the HTTP request packet. You call the InsertTodo() method from the AzureSQLDB object.

```
else
{
    string requestBody = await new StreamReader(req.Body).
    ReadToEndAsync();
    dynamic data = JsonConvert.DeserializeObject(requestBody);
    string todo = data?.message;
```

```
if(AzureSQLDB.InsertTodo(todo))
    return (ActionResult)new OkObjectResult($"succeed");
else
    return (ActionResult)new OkObjectResult($"failed");
}
```

Save all the code. Next, you deploy your Azure Functions project to the Azure server.

Deploying Your Azure Functions Project

You can deploy your project to Microsoft Azure easily through Visual Studio. You should download a publish profile file from Azure Functions. Then, you use the profile file in the project, as shown in Figure 5-8.

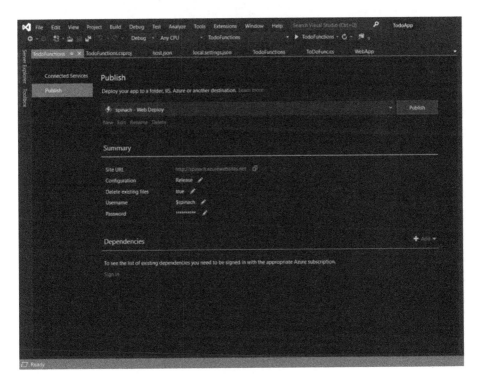

Figure 5-8. *Deploying Azure Functions to the Azure server*

115

You can also configure the project dependencies. To add Azure SQL Database, click the Add link. After clicking, you get the dialog shown in Figure 5-9. Select your existing Azure SQL Database instance.

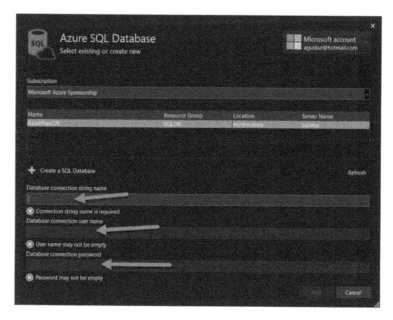

Figure 5-9. *Adding the Azure SQL Database instance to Azure Functions*

Set the database connection string name to `azure_sql`. You also need to set the username and password for Azure SQL Database. If done, click the Add button.

Now you can publish the project to Azure. Check the Application Settings area on the publishing form to see if you were successful (Figure 5-8). You should see `azure_sql` for the database connection string name, as shown in Figure 5-10.

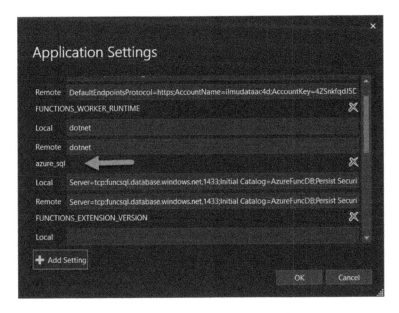

Figure 5-10. *Checking the application settings for Azure SQL Database in Azure Functions*

Next, you will test your Azure Functions program.

Testing Azure Functions

Microsoft provides an HTTP trigger for Azure Functions. You can find this tool in Azure Functions. Open Azure Functions, and you will see the "View files" and Test tabs. Click the Test tab to see the testing tool, as shown in Figure 5-11. This tool can be used to perform HTTP POST and GET requests. You also add request headers and a body.

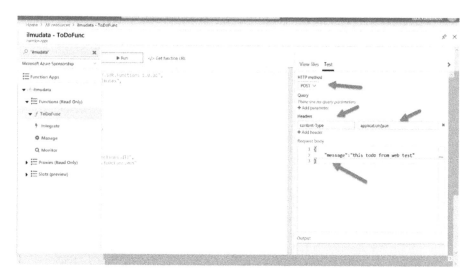

Figure 5-11. *Testing Azure Functions for the HTTP POST scenario*

For our simple scenario, you'll add a task. So, submit an HTTP POST to Azure Functions to insert a new task. You can set the HTTP method as POST. You also add a request header called content-Type with the application/json value. Then, you can write the request body as follows:

```
{
    "message": "this todo from web test"
}
```

Now you can run this tool by clicking the Run button.

After it's executed, you should get a response from Azure Functions. Testing log and output response from Azure Functions on the bottom of your tool. Figure 5-12 shows the result of our test in Azure Functions.

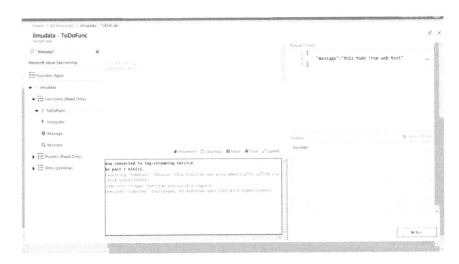

Figure 5-12. *A result of testing Azure Functions*

To verify whether your task data is stored in a database, you can use the query editor tool from Microsoft. You perform the following query by typing this script:

```
select * from dbo.todo
```

Figure 5-13 shows our the query program output.

Figure 5-13. *Verifying data on Azure SQL Database*

119

Next, you can test that Azure Functions is retrieving all the tasks by performing an HTTP GET request to Azure Functions. You don't need to put any data in the request body. After executing the request, you will see the JSON data in the Output panel, as shown in Figure 5-14.

Figure 5-14. *Testing Azure Functions for an HTTP GET scenario*

You also can perform testing using Postman. This tool can perform HTTP GET/POST requests. It's suitable for your RESTful projects. You can get this tool at `https://www.getpostman.com`.

Using the Postman tool is easy. You put in a targeted server and set up HTTP request parameters. For this scenario, you can get the Azure Functions URL from Azure Functions in the Azure portal, as shown in Figure 5-15.

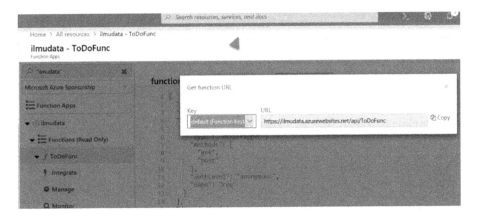

Figure 5-15. *Getting the Azure Functions URL*

For demo purposes, enter your Azure Functions URL in the Postman tool with GET mode to perform an HTTP GET. Then, click the Send button. If you succeed, you will see the response's output. Check the output data on the Body tab, as shown in Figure 5-16.

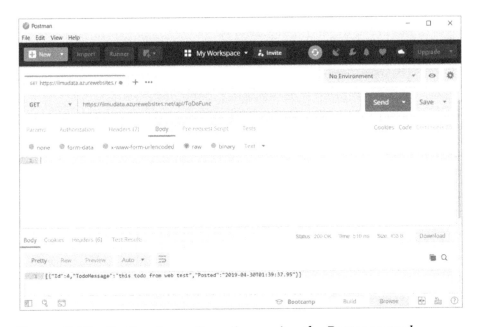

Figure 5-16. *Testing Azure Functions using the Postman tool*

After testing Azure Functions, you can continue to develop your web application in the next section.

Developing a Client Web Application

You can develop an ASP.NET Core web application to access Azure Functions. In this section, you'll use the ASP.NET MVC project template, as shown in Figure 5-17.

Next you'll add a model to the project. Add the Todo.cs file into the Models folder from your project. Then, write the following code:

```
using System;
using System.ComponentModel.DataAnnotations;

namespace TodoWebApp.Models
{
    public class Todo
    {
        public int Id { get; set; }
        [Required]
        [Display(Name = "Todo Message")]
        public string TodoMessage { get; set; }
        public DateTime Posted { get; set; }
    }
}
```

Figure 5-17. *Project structure for the web application*

Next, modify the view `Index.cshtml`. You can add your model to the
script.

```
@model TodoWebApp.Models.Todo
```

Then create a form and a table with the `<div>` tag to populate your
tasks from Azure Functions.

```
<div>
    <h4>Todo Web App</h4>
    <p>Fill your todo on this field.</p>
    <div class="form-group">
        <label class="control-label">Todo Message</label>
        <textarea id="txtMessage" class="form-control"
        rows="5" cols="20"></textarea>
    </div>
</div>
```

```
        <div class="form-group">
            <input type="button" value="Save" class="btn btn-
            primary" onclick="saveData()" />
            <label id="status"class="control-label"></label>
        </div>

    </div>
    <div class="container">
        <h2>List of Todo</h2>
        <div id="todolist" class="list-group">
        </div>
    </div>
```

The user will insert a task on Textare with an ID of txtMessage.
When the user clicks the Save button, you call the saveData() JavaScript
function. Furthermore, you populate all the tasks on the table <div> with
an ID of todolist. This task data is populated from JavaScript scripts. You
implement the JavaScript scripts at the bottom of the <HTML> tag.

First, you call the reloadTodo() JavaScript function when the page
document is loaded. You retrieve all the tasks from Azure Functions
by calling the jQuery get() function. This function performs an HTTP
GET. Here we are passing https://ilmudata.azurewebsites.net/api/
ToDoFunc to Azure Functions. Change it to your own Azure Functions URL.

```
<script>
    $(document).ready(function () {
        $('#status').html("");
        reloadTodo();
    });

    function reloadTodo() {
        $.get("https://ilmudata.azurewebsites.net/api/ToDoFunc",
            function (data) {
```

```
            console.log(data);
            $.each(JSON.parse(data), function (i, item) {
                $('<a href="#" class="list-group-item"><h4
                class="list-group-item-heading">' + item.
                TodoMessage +
                '</h4><p class="list-group-item-text">' +
                item.Posted +
                    '</p></a>').appendTo("#todolist");
            });

        });
    }
```

You also implement the saveData() JavaScript function to store a task into Azure SQL Database. You get a task name using jQuery. Then, you post a task data in JSON format to Azure Functions using the post() function from jQuery. Change the Azure Functions URL to your own.

```
function saveData() {
    var txt = $('textarea#txtMessage').val();
    var data = {
        message: txt
    };

    $.post("https://ilmudata.azurewebsites.net/api/ToDoFunc",
        JSON.stringify(data),
        function (result) {
            console.log(result);
            if (result == "succeed") {
                $('#status').html("Saving data was succeed");
                $('textarea#txtMessage').val(");
                reloadTodo();
```

```
            } else {
                $('#status').html("Saving data was failed");
            }
        });
    }
</script>
```

Since you use jQuery in the ASP.NET Core view, you should modify the _Layout.cshtml file so the jQuery file is loaded in the HTML header. You can modify it as shown here:

```
<head>
    <meta charset="utf-8" />
    <meta name="viewport" content="width=device-width, initial-
    scale=1.0" />
    <title>@ViewData["Title"] - Todo WebApp</title>

    <script src="https://cdnjs.cloudflare.com/ajax/libs/
    jquery/3.3.1/jquery.min.js"
            asp-fallback-src="~/lib/jquery/dist/jquery.min.js"
            asp-fallback-test="window.jQuery"
            crossorigin="anonymous"
            integrity="sha256-FgpCb/KJQlLNfOu91ta32o/
            NMZxltwRo8QtmkMRdAu8=">
    </script>
</head>
```

Save your code now.

Now you can run the ASP.NET Core application. Write your task and then click the Save button. You should get a confirmation. You also get a list of existing tasks. Figure 5-18 shows our program output in the ASP.NET Core web application.

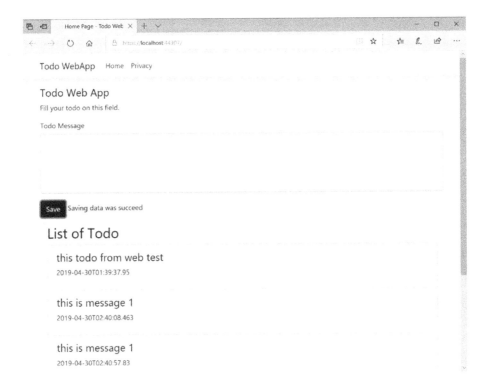

Figure 5-18. *Program output in ASP.NET Core web application*

If you get errors regarding CORS, you can set Azure Functions to enable CORS operations. You can find the setting on the "Platform features" tab in Azure Functions, as shown in Figure 5-19. Add your web URL from the ASP.NET Core web application.

Figure 5-19. *Configuring CORS in Azure Functions*

Summary

In this chapter, you learned how to access Azure Functions from a web application. You also developed a simple project by implementing an Azure Functions program, a web application, and an Azure SQL Database instance. In the next chapter, you will focus on how to work with Azure Functions and mobile applications.

CHAPTER 6

Mobile Back End

Mobile applications have been one of the greatest innovations of the Internet era. Many businesses provide mobile applications to increase sales or drive business to their company. This chapter explores how to integrate mobile applications with Azure Functions. Essentially, Azure Functions works as the back end to serve a mobile application.

The following topics are covered in this chapter:

- Mobile platforms

- Using Azure Functions for mobile applications

- Building an Azure Functions program for an Android application

Reviewing Mobile Platforms

Nowadays people can't get away from their mobile devices. People use the mobile applications on their mobile devices to increase their productivity. Others use mobile applications to have fun such as when playing mobile game applications.

There are two mainstream platforms for mobile applications, Android and iOS. Android is built by Google, and iOS is built by Apple. Each mobile platform provides an application store so that people can download and install mobile applications. Some applications are free, and others cost money.

© Agus Kurniawan, Wely Lau 2019
A. Kurniawan and W. Lau, *Practical Azure Functions*,
https://doi.org/10.1007/978-1-4842-5067-9_6

To develop an Android application, you need to register as an Android developer. All the development tools are free. You can get all the Android resources at `https://developer.android.com`. To publish your Android application to the Google Play Store, you have to pay Google. Currently, the cost is $25 for a lifetime. Google provides an Android emulator to test your program, so you don't need to get an Android device to run your program. Still, it's recommended that you have an Android device to make sure your Android application runs well on a real device.

To develop an iOS application, you can use Objective-C and Swift. You also need a Mac to develop iOS programs. To access the iOS development resources, you need a developer license from Apple. Currently, the Apple developer license is $99 per year. You can get more information about registering to be an Apple developer at `https://developer.apple.com`.

Sometimes you need to maintain Android and iOS versions of your mobile application. This has been a painful experience, but there is another option, which is to use hybrid approach. You can use the Ionic (`https://ionicframework.com`) and React Native `https://facebook.github.io/react-native/` (frameworks). These frameworks use HTML5 as the programming language. If you love C#, you can choose Xamarin to develop Android and iOS applications. You can get more information about Xamarin development on `https://visualstudio.microsoft.com/xamarin/` website.

In this chapter, we focus on the Android platform when creating a mobile application to access Azure Functions.

Introducing Azure Functions for Mobile Applications

Microsoft provides an Azure solution to enable you to work with various mobile platforms. You can host app services to serve your mobile requests over HTTP/HTTPS. You can also build mobile notifications to create more interactions between your application and users. You can see a list of

Azure services that you can use in mobile applications at `https://azure.microsoft.com/en-us/product-categories/mobile/`. Figure 6-1 shows the various Azure services for mobile applications.

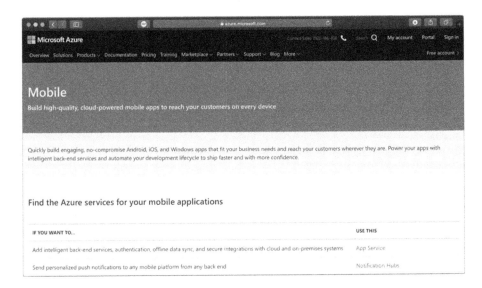

Figure 6-1. *Azure services for mobile applications*

Azure Functions is one of the Azure services that enables you to serve your mobile applications. Azure Functions can work as a "service interface" so you can access internal Azure resources such as Azure SQL Database, Azure Storage, and other compute resources. Azure Functions with an HTTP trigger can be used as the interface to your back end for mobile applications. In this chapter, you'll explore how to access Azure Functions from mobile applications.

First, you'll develop an Android application that works with Azure Functions. Specifically, you'll learn how to make a registration application on Android.

Building a Registration Mobile Application

In this section, you'll learn how to develop a mobile application to access Azure Functions. For the mobile platform implementation, we will use the Android platform. Azure Functions will perform the user registration process. All Android requests will be handled by Azure Functions. Figure 6-2 shows the demo scenario. The Android application will send the user registration data to the Microsoft Azure server through Azure Functions. You'll also prepare Azure Functions to listen for incoming messages via the HTTP POST protocol. Once Azure Functions receives data, Azure Functions will store the data in Azure SQL Database.

Figure 6-2. *A demo scenario of a mobile application and Azure Functions*

To implement the demo, you should have an active account on Microsoft Azure. Some Azure resources will probably cost money, such as Azure SQL Database.

Next, you'll create an Azure SQL Database instance.

Creating an Azure SQL Database Instance

All the user registration data will be stored in Azure SQL Database. Azure SQL Database uses SQL Server running in a cloud environment. You can find detailed service information and a list of the features of Azure SQL Database at https://azure.microsoft.com/en-us/services/sql-database/.

Now you'll create a database on Azure SQL Database or use your existing Azure SQL Database instance. Figure 6-3 shows the dashboard for Azure SQL Database. You can see our `funcsql` server has a database called `azurefuncdb` on it.

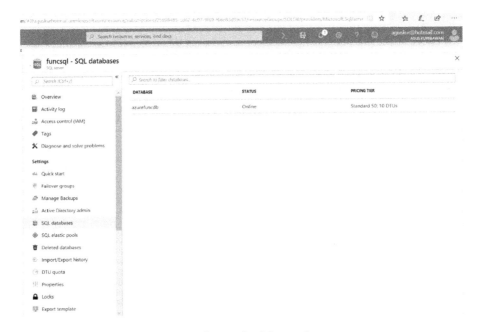

Figure 6-3. *Azure SQL Database dashboard*

Next, you'll create a table for demo purposes using SQL scripting. To keep the data model simple, the user registration application has two data items: full name and e-mail. You'll name the table `UserReg`, and it will have four columns, as follows:

- `id` is a primary key of the `UserReg` table.

- `fullname` is the full name of the user.

- `email` is the user's e-mail.

- `posted` is a date of the received data.

Create the UserReg table using the following SQL script:

```
CREATE TABLE [dbo].[UserReg](
     [id] [int] IDENTITY(1,1) NOT NULL,
     [fullname] [varchar](50) NOT NULL,
     [email] [varchar](30) NOT NULL,
     [posted] [datetime] NOT NULL,
 CONSTRAINT [PK_UserReg] PRIMARY KEY CLUSTERED
(
     [id] ASC
)WITH (PAD_INDEX = OFF, STATISTICS_NORECOMPUTE = OFF, IGNORE_
DUP_KEY = OFF, ALLOW_ROW_LOCKS = ON, ALLOW_PAGE_LOCKS = ON) ON
[PRIMARY]
) ON [PRIMARY]
GO
```

You can run these scripts in the query editor available on the database dashboard in your Azure SQL Database instance. You can also run this script using SQL Server Management Studio with remoting to the Azure SQL Database server. Figure 6-4 shows the UserReg table on our database.

Figure 6-4. *Creating the UserReg table in Azure SQL Database*

Next, you can create an Azure Functions project using Visual Studio to serve all the requests from Android applications.

Creating an Azure Functions Project

Azure Functions is designed to be easy to use. You can develop an Azure Functions program using the Azure web editor or using Visual Studio. You also can create an Azure Functions program with the Azure CLI. In this section, you'll learn how to develop an Azure Functions program using Visual Studio 2019.

You can start creating the Azure Functions project by selecting the Azure Functions template. Since we're talking about Android applications in this chapter, use the HTTP trigger template to start your Azure Functions program, as shown in Figure 6-5. An Android application can communicate over HTTP easily.

You'll want to set up a storage account for your project. Set the access rights to Anonymous. Fill in the project name; we used **RegAzureFunctions**. After filling in all the project fields, click the OK button.

Figure 6-5. *Creating an Azure Functions project with an HTTP trigger*

You will get some template code for your Azure Functions project. Before you write any new code, you need to add the prerequisite libraries. So, add the `System.Data.SqlClient` and `Newtonsoft.Json` libraries to your project through NuGet.

This program scenario is to listen for an HTTP trigger. You will receive a message from an Android application in JSON format in the following format:

```
{
    "fullname": "<full name of user>",
    "email":"<user email>"
}
```

You can encode this JSON message from the HTTP body request and convert it to a UserReg object via the deserialization process by calling the JsonConvert.DeserializeObject() method. This method is part of the Newtonsoft.Json library. After obtaining the UserReg object, Azure Functions will store it in Azure SQL Database.

The UserReg object holds the full name and e-mail of the user. You define the UserReg object as the UserReg.cs file. The following is the UserReg object implementation:

```
using System;

namespace RegAzureFunctions
{
    public class UserReg
    {
        public string FullName { set; get; }
        public string Email { set; get; }
    }
}
```

To continue the example, we store the UserReg object in Azure SQL Database and define your own database object, called AzureSQLDB. Then call the InsertRegistration() method to store the data in the database.

The following is the Azure Functions code implementation:

```
[FunctionName("RegAzureFunc")]
public static async Task<IActionResult> Run(
    [HttpTrigger(AuthorizationLevel.Anonymous, "post", Route =
    null)] HttpRequest req,
    ILogger log)
{
    log.LogInformation("C# HTTP trigger function processed a
    request.");
```

```
string requestBody = await new StreamReader(req.Body).
ReadToEndAsync();
UserReg user = JsonConvert.DeserializeObject<UserReg>(reque
stBody);

return AzureSQLDB.InsertRegistration(user)
    ? (ActionResult)new OkObjectResult($"Registration data
    was received")
    : new BadRequestObjectResult("There was error to save
    data into Azure SQL Database");
}
```

The AzureSQLDB object applies ADO.NET objects to manipulate data for SQL Server. You define the InsertRegistration() method to store data in Azure SQL Database, and you use the SQLCommand object to execute the INSERT query to store the database by calling the ExecuteNonQuery() method and passing the UserReg object.

```
public static bool InsertRegistration(UserReg user)
{
    string db = Environment.GetEnvironmentVariable("azure_sql");

    try
    {
        using (SqlConnection conn = new SqlConnection(db))
        {
            conn.Open();
            var text = "INSERT INTO [UserReg]
            (fullname,email,posted) " +
                "VALUES(@fullname,@email,getdate())";
```

```
        using (SqlCommand cmd = new SqlCommand(text, conn))
        {
            cmd.Parameters.Add(new SqlParameter
            ("@fullname", user.FullName));
            cmd.Parameters.Add(new SqlParameter("@email",
            user.Email));

            cmd.ExecuteNonQuery();

        }
    }
}
catch (Exception)
{
    return false;
}

return true;
}
```

You can obtain a connection string for Azure SQL Database from the azure_sql setting, which you define when publishing your Azure Functions project to Microsoft Azure. Now you can compile your Azure Functions project. Make sure you don't get any errors while compiling the project.

So, you have developed an Azure Functions project using Visual Studio. Next, you will publish it.

Publishing an Azure Functions Program

Publishing an Azure Functions project with Visual Studio is easy. Right-click the Azure Functions project and then select the Publish menu. You can publish the project by logging in with your existing Azure account, or you can import the Azure Functions profile file from Azure Functions.

For this demo, you will publish your project into the existing Azure Functions account by selecting your existing Azure App Service account and then choosing your Azure Functions service, as shown in Figure 6-6. Click the OK button when you're done.

Figure 6-6. *Choosing an existing Azure Functions profile*

After selecting the Azure profile for Azure Functions, you will see the publishing settings, as shown in Figure 6-7. Next, you can configure a connection string for Azure SQL Database.

Specifically, you should define the `azure_sql` setting for your project. You can copy the database connection string from Azure SQL Database by clicking the Edit Azure App service setting menu in Figure 6-7. Then, paste it into `azure_sql` in the Remote field, as shown in Figure 6-8. When you're done, click the OK button to save these publishing settings.

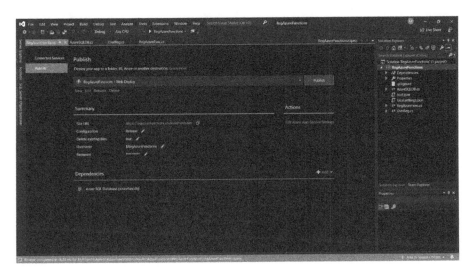

Figure 6-7. *Publish settings in Azure Functions project*

After you successfully publish, you will be able to see your Azure Functions program in the Azure Functions dashboard. Next, you will test your Azure Functions program.

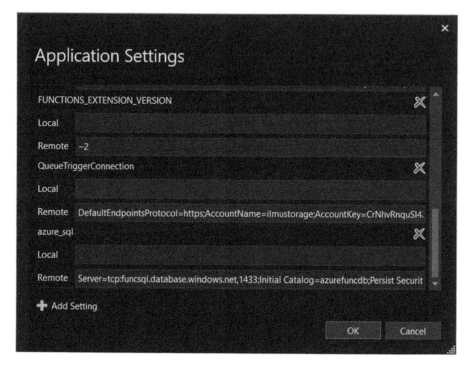

Figure 6-8. *Configuring a database connection for Azure SQL Database*

Testing an Azure Functions Program

You can test Azure Functions programs using the web tool from Azure. First you open your Azure Functions program on the Azure Functions dashboard. Then you click the Test tab so you can see the testing features, as shown in Figure 6-9. For this demo, you can send some dummy registration data in JSON format. Write this JSON data in the request body:

```
{
    "fullname": "agus kurniawan",
    "email":"agusk@myemail.com"

}
```

Click the Run button to execute this tool. You should see verbose messages during testing in the Logs window, as shown in Figure 6-9. You also can see the response messages from the Azure Functions server in the Logs window.

Figure 6-9. *Testing Azure Functions programs using the Azure Functions web tool*

After sending data to Azure Functions, you can verify your data in Azure SQL Database. Open your database in Azure SQL Database. Then, perform a SQL query to see your data. You should see the data that was sent from the web test tool. Figure 6-10 shows our resulting data in Azure SQL Database.

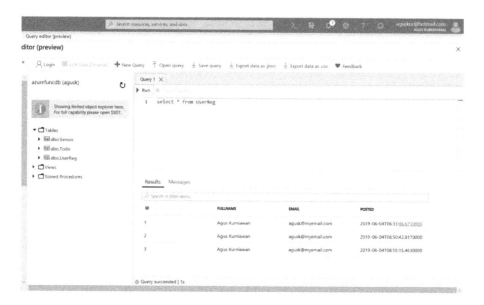

Figure 6-10. *Displaying UserReg data using the query editor in Azure SQL Database*

Next, you will learn how to develop an Android program to access an Azure Functions program.

Developing an Android Application

You have developed an Azure Functions program and have already uploaded it to Microsoft Azure. Now you can develop a program for an Android application. For the development tool, you can use Android Studio from Google. You can download and install it at `https://developer.android.com/studio`.

Microsoft has provided SDK libraries for mobile platforms. For the Android platform, you can use the Android SDK to access Azure services using the `Azure.Android` SDK. Visit `https://github.com/Azure/Azure.Android` to get the details.

For this demo, you will see how to develop an Android program using Android Studio. You could also develop an Android program using Java or Kotlin. For this demo, we're using Java as the programming language to build the Android application.

Open Android Studio and select the Empty activity template. Fill in your project name; for instance, we entered **RegistrationApp**, as shown in Figure 6-11. Click the Finish button to create your Android project.

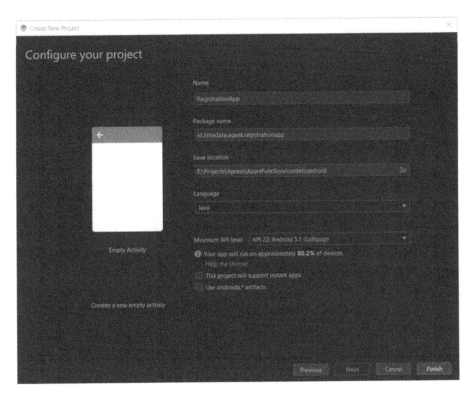

Figure 6-11. *Creating an Android project using Android Studio*

Now you'll start to develop the UI. You can open activity_main. xml and build the UI, as shown in Figure 6-12. You need two EditText components to hold the full name and e-mail data.

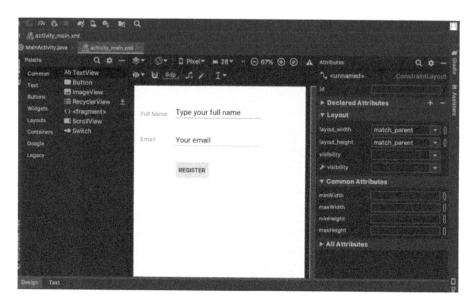

Figure 6-12. *Designing the Android UI*

Now you can write the Android program. Since you access Azure Functions with HTTP triggers, you don't need to use the Azure SDK directly. You can use any Android library to access HTTP/HTTPS. For this demo, you'll use the Volley library to perform HTTP accesses. You can get further information about Volley at `https://developer.android.com/training/volley`.

To work with the Volley library, you can add this library on `build. gradle` for the app. You add this library in `dependencies{}` as follows:

```
dependencies {
    ...
    implementation 'com.android.volley:volley:1.1.1'
}
```

You add the logic for the program by clicking the Register button. First, you can obtain the full name and e-mail from the `EditText` components. Then, you construct JSON data to be sent to Azure Functions. You also

define the URL for Azure Functions to put in the url variable. You can get
the Azure Functions URL from the Azure Functions dashboard. Open your
Azure Functions program and then click "Get function URL," as shown
in Figure 6-13. Put this value into the url variable. You also construct
RequestQueue from the Volley object.

```
try {
    EditText fullName = (EditText) findViewById(R.id.txtFullName);
    EditText email = (EditText) findViewById(R.id.txtEmail);

    RequestQueue queue = Volley.newRequestQueue(this);

    final String url = "https://regazurefunctions.
azurewebsites.net/api/RegAzureFunc";
    JSONObject jsonBody = new JSONObject();
    jsonBody.put("fullname", fullName.getText());
    jsonBody.put("email", email.getText());
    final String requestBody = jsonBody.toString();
```

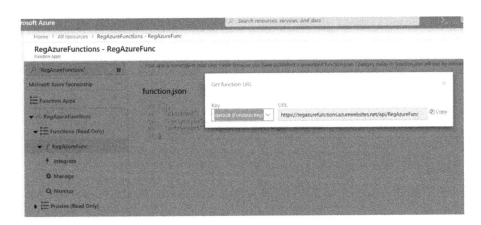

Figure 6-13. *Getting the Azure Functions URL*

147

Next, send your JSON data to the Azure Functions server. You can use Volley to implement the sending process. You construct the StringRequest object to listen for onRensponse() and ErrorListener(). Write all the information into the Log object so you can monitor these messages.

```
StringRequest postRequest = new StringRequest(Request.Method.
POST, url,
        new Response.Listener<String>()
        {
            @Override
            public void onResponse(String response) {
                // response
                Log.i("VOLLEY", response);
            }
        },

        new Response.ErrorListener()
        {
            @Override
            public void onErrorResponse(VolleyError error) {
                // error
                Log.e("VOLLEY", error.getMessage());
            }
        }
```

Override some methods on StringRequest such as getBodyContentType() to set JSON as the body content type. You also override the getBody() method to send your JSON data into the Volley object.

```
) {
    @Override
    public String getBodyContentType() {
        return "application/json; charset=utf-8";
    }
    @Override
    public byte[] getBody() throws AuthFailureError {
        try {
            return requestBody == null ? null : requestBody.
            getBytes("utf-8");
        } catch (UnsupportedEncodingException uee) {
            VolleyLog.wtf("Unsupported Encoding while trying to
            get the bytes of %s using %s", requestBody, "utf-8");
            return null;
        }
    }
    @Override
    protected Response<String> parseNetworkResponse(NetworkResp
    onse response) {
        String responseString = "";
        if (response != null) {
            responseString = String.valueOf(response.statusCode);
            // can get more details such as response.headers
        }
        return Response.success(responseString,
        HttpHeaderParser.parseCacheHeaders(response));
    }
};
```

Now pass the StringRequest object into the RequestQueue object. You also show a notification to the user using the Toast object. You catch all errors with try-catch in your code.

```
    queue.add(postRequest);

    Toast.makeText(getApplicationContext(),
            "Data was sent to Azure Queue", Toast.LENGTH_SHORT)
            .show();
}
catch (Exception e) {
    Toast.makeText(getApplicationContext(),
            e.getMessage(), Toast.LENGTH_SHORT)
            .show();
}
```

Last, set the permission for your Android app to be able to work on the Internet. Put this in the AndroidManifest.xml file:

```
<uses-permission android:name="android.permission.INTERNET" />
```

Save all your code. Now you can build and run this program to the Android emulator, as shown in Figure 6-14. Fill in the full name and e-mail. Then, click the Register button to send the data to Azure Functions. Make sure your Android emulator has Internet access to enable users to submit data to Azure Functions.

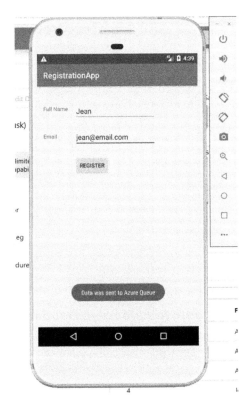

Figure 6-14. *Android application accessing Azure Functions*

After clicking, you can check Azure SQL Database. You should see your data in Azure SQL Database. You can perform a SELECT query on the UserReg table. Figure 6-15 shows the data that we sent to Azure SQL Database.

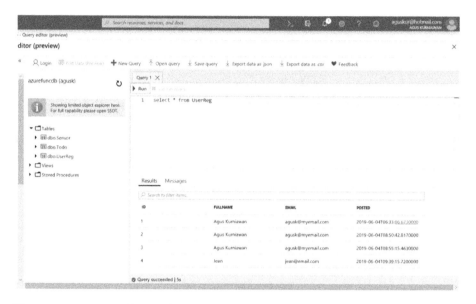

Figure 6-15. *Verifying data in Azure SQL Database*

Summary

In this chapter, you learned how to access Azure Functions from an Android application. You also developed a simple project, a user registration application, by integrating Azure Functions and Azure SQL Database.

In the next chapter, you will learn how to build microservices by applying Azure Functions.

CHAPTER 7

Serverless Microservices

Microservices provide scalability and availability for applications. Developing a microservice means you are developing a loosely coupled system and your application will be split into various services. In this chapter, you'll explore how to build microservices with Azure Functions.

The following topics are covered in this chapter:

- Introduction to microservices

- How to implement microservices with Azure Functions

- How to develop and test microservices

Introducing Microservices

If you are a web developer, you probably have built a web application with a database server. Some developers apply a tiers approach when developing web applications. Figure 7-1 shows the general design of a web application. The core business process is built in the business layer, and the data layer is used to manage the data going to the database servers.

© Agus Kurniawan, Wely Lau 2019
A. Kurniawan and W. Lau, *Practical Azure Functions*,
https://doi.org/10.1007/978-1-4842-5067-9_7

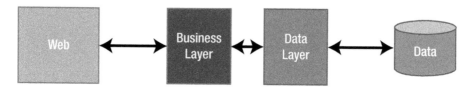

Figure 7-1. *A general design for a web application*

When the number of users accessing a web application increases, you'll usually scale your web application. If your web application uses a tiers approach, your design is a tightly coupled system. This means you can scale your business and data layers.

One solution uses multiple distributions of a web application. You can design the scalability of a web application as shown in Figure 7-2. In this scenario, you deploy different web application instances on different computer machines or virtual machines.

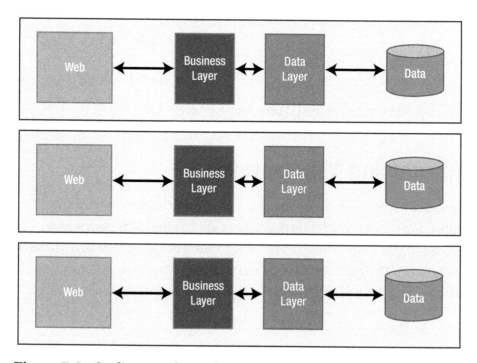

Figure 7-2. *Scaling a web application*

One of the disadvantages of the tiers approach to a web application is that it is not easy to manage the data and sessions. When you change the code in the business layer, you have to deploy the revised web application to all the servers.

Another solution is to scale the web application to use microservices. In this way, you separate some services from the tiers architecture. Each service has its own business logic and data. In general, you can migrate the web application tier-based model to the microservices model, as shown in Figure 7-3. Each service can take care of the user data. With microservices, you can work with different versions among services.

In this chapter, you will learn how to develop microservices using Microsoft Azure and Azure Functions. You will create a simple demo for handling simple transactions.

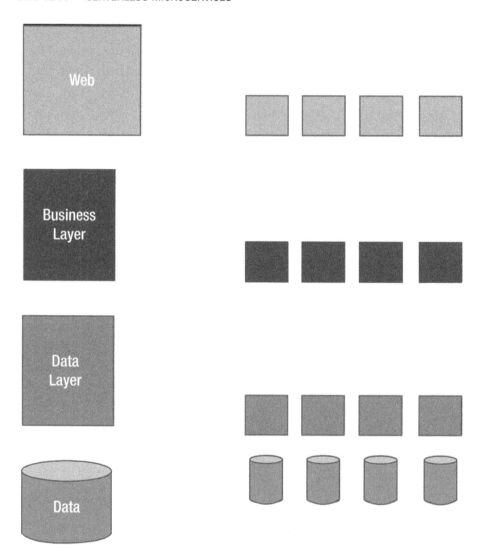

Figure 7-3. *Migrating a web application to a microservices architecture*

In this chapter, we will focus on developing microservices with Microsoft Azure and Azure Functions.

Implementing Microservices with Azure Functions

We have reviewed the basics of microservices. Now you will learn how to implement microservices with Microsoft Azure. In general, you can build microservices with Microsoft Azure easily. In fact, Microsoft provides various cloud services to develop microservices; everything from application services to database services can be used in your microservices design. You can combine some Azure resources as microservice applications. Application state data can be stored in Azure Storage or Azure Database.

You can use Azure Service Fabric to implement a microservices solution. You can create, deploy, and manage various containers in Azure Service Fabric. You can review this service at `https://azure.microsoft.com/en-in/services/service-fabric`. If you have a plan to build microservices using Azure Functions, you can put the business program into Azure Functions. To handle states and data, you can use Azure Storage, Azure SQL Database, or other Azure storage services.

Furthermore, you can review some Azure services to build a microservices application. Microsoft has provided some guidelines for microservices development at `https://docs.microsoft.com/en-us/azure/architecture/microservices/`.

Next, you'll see how to build a demo to develop microservices with Azure Functions. Specifically, you'll make a simple order application.

Building a Microservices System with Azure Functions

In this section, you'll develop a microservices application with Azure Functions. The application will serve orders from HTTP web services and Azure Storage. Figure 7-4 shows the demo scenario. An order can be made by

157

calling HTTP services and Azure Storage. The application can call HTTP POST to make a transaction. This process will be handled by Azure Functions. Azure Functions will put this order into Azure Queue. Other applications also can make a transaction by putting an order into Azure Queue directly.

Once an order is received by Azure Queue, your Azure Functions application can pick up and process the transaction. All transactions will be stored in Azure SQL Database.

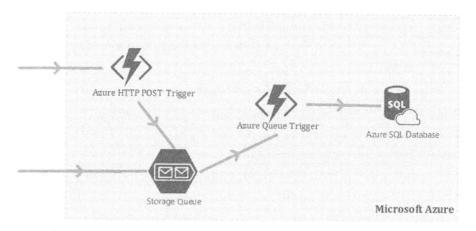

Figure 7-4. *A demo scenario for microservices with Azure Functions*

To implement this demo, you should have an active account on Microsoft Azure. Some Azure resources probably will cost money such as Azure SQL Database.

Next, you'll create an Azure SQL Database instance.

Creating an Azure SQL Database Instance

All transactions are stored in Azure SQL Database. You can learn more about the Azure SQL Database service at `https://azure.microsoft.com/en-us/services/sql-database/`. You can create a new database server or use an existing database. For instance, in this example, we're creating a database called `azurefuncdb`.

Next, you'll create a table for example purposes using SQL scripting. For a simple data model, your order transaction has four data items: product name, price, quantity, and buyer. So, you'll define a table called FuncOrder with these four columns:

- id is a primary key of the FuncOrder table.
- productname is a product name.
- price is the product price.
- quantity is the quantity of the product order.
- buyer is the name of the buyer.
- posted is the date of the received data.

You can create the FuncOrder table using the following SQL:

```
CREATE TABLE [dbo].[FuncOrder](
      [id] [int] IDENTITY(1,1) NOT NULL,
      [productname] [varchar](30) NOT NULL,
      [price] [numeric] NOT NULL,
      [quantity] [int] NOT NULL,
      [buyer] [varchar](15) NOT NULL,
      [posted] [datetime] NOT NULL,
 CONSTRAINT [PK_FuncOrder] PRIMARY KEY CLUSTERED
(
      [id] ASC
)WITH (PAD_INDEX = OFF, STATISTICS_NORECOMPUTE = OFF, IGNORE_
DUP_KEY = OFF, ALLOW_ROW_LOCKS = ON, ALLOW_PAGE_LOCKS = ON) ON
[PRIMARY]
) ON [PRIMARY]
GO
```

You can run these scripts in the query editor from the database dashboard in Azure SQL Database, or you can run this script using SQL Server Management Studio with remoting to the Azure SQL Database server.

159

Next, you'll create an Azure Functions project to serve all the requests from Android applications.

Creating an Azure Functions Project

In this section, you'll develop an Azure Functions project. As shown in Figure 7-4, you will create two Azure Functions in one project using Visual Studio 2019. Create a new project with the Azure Functions template with .NET Core.

Since you have two Azure Functions functions, you can use two Azure Functions with HTTP Trigger and Queue Trigger templates. Name them **OrderHttpApi** for the HTTP trigger and **OrderProcFunc** for the queue trigger.

Next, you'll need to add some required libraries into your project. Specifically, add the following required libraries via NuGet:

- Microsoft.Azure.Storage.Queue

- Microsoft.Azure.WebJobs.Extensions.Storage

- Newtonsoft.Json

- System.Configuration.ConfigurationManager

- System.Data.SqlClient

Next, create a domain object, called FuncOrder, that holds order data. Create a file called FuncOrder.cs and then write the following code:

```
using System;

namespace MicroFunctions
{
    public class FuncOrder
    {
        public int Id { get; set; }
        public string ProductName { get; set; }
```

```
        public float Price { get; set; }
        public int Quantity { get; set; }
        public string Buyer { get; set; }
    }
}
```

You can use the FuncOrder object to map your database table, FuncOrder. To handle data processing from Azure Functions to Azure SQL Database, you create an AzureSQLDB object. Perform a query to insert data into Azure SQL Database. For the implementation, you can create a file called AzureSQLDB.cs in your project. First, you define your required libraries, as shown here:

```
using System;
using System.Data.SqlClient;
```

Next, you create a method, InsertNewOrder(), to insert data into Azure SQL Database. For the database configuration, you read it from the azure_sql parameter. To insert data into Azure SQL Database, you can use an ADO.NET approach by using SQLConnection and SQLCommand to perform SQL queries.

The InsertNewOrder() method receives a FuncOrder object that will be inserted into Azure SQL Database. The following is the complete code for the InsertNewOrder() method:

```
public class AzureSQLDB
{
public static bool InsertNewOrder(FuncOrder order)
{
    string db = Environment.GetEnvironmentVariable("azure_sql");

    try
    {
        using (SqlConnection conn = new SqlConnection(db))
```

```
        {
            conn.Open();
            var text = "INSERT INTO [FuncOrder](productname,
            price,quantity,buyer,posted) " +
                "VALUES(@productname,@price,@quantity,
                @buyer,getdate())";

            using (SqlCommand cmd = new SqlCommand(text, conn))
            {
                cmd.Parameters.Add(new SqlParameter
                ("@productname",order.ProductName));
                cmd.Parameters.Add(new SqlParameter
                ("@price", order.Price));
                cmd.Parameters.Add(new SqlParameter
                ("@quantity", order.Quantity));
                cmd.Parameters.Add(new SqlParameter
                ("@buyer", order.Buyer));

                cmd.ExecuteNonQuery();

            }
        }
    }
    catch (Exception)
    {
        return false;
    }

    return true;
}
```

Now you will continue to develop the Azure Functions project. There are two functions, OrderHttpApi for the HTTP trigger and OrderProcFunc for the queue trigger. First, let's implement OrderHttpApi. This function listens to HTTP POST from clients. Once you receive HTTP POST data, you parse the request body to be sent to Azure Storage Queue. You declare your Azure Storage Queue libraries as follows:

```
using Microsoft.Azure.Storage; // Namespace for
                                        CloudStorageAccount
using Microsoft.Azure.Storage.Queue; // Namespace for Queue
                                        storage types
```

Then, you set Anonymous for the authorization level so you can receive all HTTP POST requests without performing authentication and authorization. After receiving the HTTP POST data, you send it to Azure Storage Queue using the CloudQueue object with the order-queue name. You call AddMessage() by passing the CloudQueueMessage object. A configuration string for Azure Storage Queue is obtained from the storage_queue configuration parameter. You will set it while deploying the project. You can configure it in the Azure Functions dashboard.

The following is the complete code for OrderHttpApi:

```
public static class OrderHttpApi
{
    [FunctionName("OrderHttpApi")]
    public static async Task<IActionResult> Run(
        [HttpTrigger(AuthorizationLevel.Anonymous, "post",
        Route = null)] HttpRequest req,
        ILogger log)
    {
        log.LogInformation("C# HTTP trigger function processed
        a request.");

        string requestBody = await new StreamReader(req.Body).
        ReadToEndAsync();
        if(!string.IsNullOrEmpty(requestBody))
        {
```

```
    string storageConnection = Environment.
    GetEnvironmentVariable("storage_queue");
    CloudStorageAccount storageAccount =
    CloudStorageAccount.Parse(storageConnection);

    CloudQueueClient qc = storageAccount.
    CreateCloudQueueClient();
    CloudQueue queue = qc.GetQueueReference("order-
    queue");

    queue.CreateIfNotExists();
    CloudQueueMessage message = new CloudQueueMessage
    (requestBody);
    queue.AddMessage(message);

    return (ActionResult)new OkObjectResult($"Succeed");

}
else
    return new BadRequestObjectResult("Please order
    data in the request body");

    }
}
```

Now you'll implement the OrderProcFunc function. At first, you declare the following:

```
using Newtonsoft.Json;
using System.Configuration;
```

You will listen for incoming queue messages on the order-queue queue. Once you receive a message, you can validate it by deserializing with the DeserializeObject<> method. The result of the deserialization process is the FuncOrder object. You insert this object into Azure SQL Database using the AzureSQLDB object that you already created.

The following is the complete code for OrderProcFunc:

```
public static class OrderProcFunc
{
    [FunctionName("OrderProcFunc")]
    public static void Run([QueueTrigger("order-queue",
    Connection = "storage_queue")]string queueItem, ILogger log)
    {
        log.LogInformation($"C# Queue trigger function
        processed: {queueItem}");
        if (queueItem.Length > 0)
        {
            // save into database
            FuncOrder order = JsonConvert.DeserializeObject<Fun
            cOrder>(queueItem);
            if (AzureSQLDB.InsertNewOrder(order))
                log.LogInformation($"Data was saved into Azure
                SQL Database");
            else
                log.LogInformation($"There was error to save
                data into Azure SQL Database");
        }
        else
        {
            log.LogInformation($"No data was saved into Azure
            SQL Database");
        }
    }
}
```

A connection string for Azure SQL Database is obtained from the azure_sql setting. You can define the azure_sql setting when publishing Azure Functions to Microsoft Azure. Now you can compile your Azure Functions project. Make sure you don't obtain errors while compiling the project.

So, you have developed Azure Functions using Visual Studio. Next, you will publish them.

Publishing Azure Functions

Publishing Azure Functions projects with Visual Studio is easy. Right-click the Azure Functions project and then select the Publish menu. You can publish your project by logging in with your existing Azure account or import the Azure Functions profile file from Azure Functions.

After selecting the Azure profile for Azure Functions, you obtain the publishing settings. Next, you also configure a connection string for Azure Storage Queue and Azure SQL Database.

You should define the azure_sql setting on your project. You can get a database connection string from Azure SQL Database. Copy a connection string from Azure SQL Database. Click the Edit Azure App service setting menu in Figure 7-5.

Figure 7-5. *Publish settings in Azure Functions project*

You set a connection string for Azure Storage named **storage_queue**
(Figure 7-5), which you can get from the "Access keys" age in Azure
Storage, as shown in Figure 7-6. You can copy and paste it on
storage_queue (Figure 7-5). When you're done, click the OK button to
save these publishing settings.

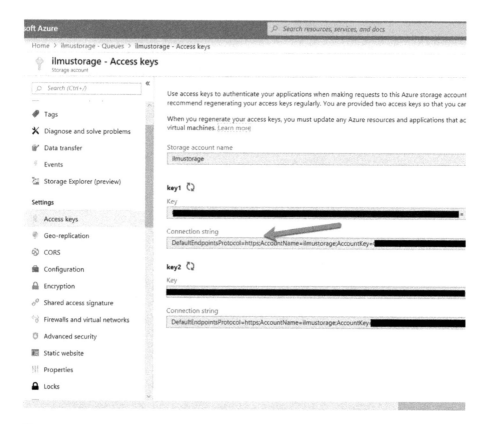

Figure 7-6. *Getting a connection string from Azure Storage Queue*

After you publish, you can see your functions in the Azure Functions dashboard, as shown in Figure 7-7. Next, you will test your Azure Functions project.

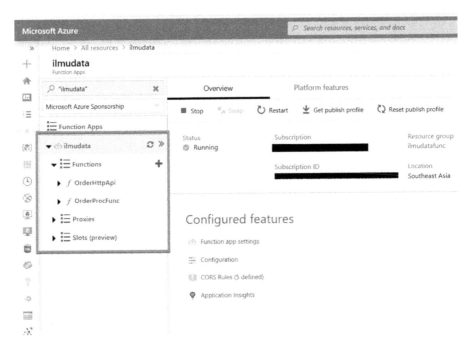

Figure 7-7. *Two deployed functions*

Testing the OrderHttpApi Function

You can test your OrderHttpApi function using the web tool from Azure.
Open your OrderHttpApi function in the Azure Functions dashboard.
Click the Test tab so you can see the test tool, as shown in Figure 7-8. For
your demo, you can send some dummy order data in JSON format. You
can write this JSON data in the request body.

```
{
  "productname":"product A",
  "price": 2.55,
  "quantity": 3,
  "buyer":"jane"
}
```

You can click the Run button to execute this tool. Technically, you will see verbose messages during testing in the Logs window, as shown in Figure 7-8. You also can see the response messages from the Azure Functions server in the Logs window.

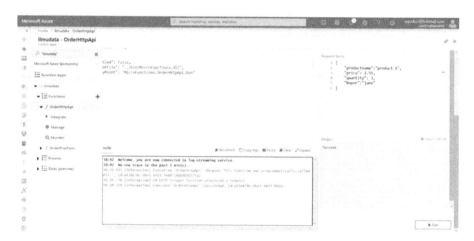

Figure 7-8. *Testing Azure Functions using the Azure Functions web tool*

After sending data to the OrderHttpApi function, you can verify your data in Azure SQL Database. Open your database in Azure SQL Database. Then, perform a SQL query to see your data. You should see your data that was sent from the web test tool. Figure 7-9 shows the result data in Azure SQL Database.

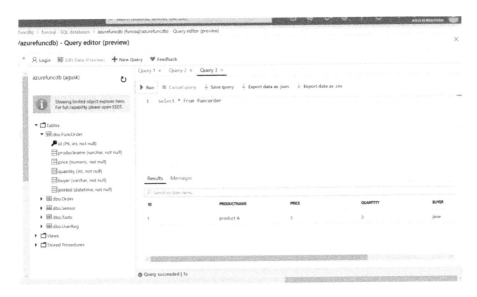

Figure 7-9. *Displaying FuncOrder data using the query editor in Azure SQL Database*

Next, you will test the OrderProcFunc function.

Sending Orders to Azure Storage Queue

You have tested your project by sending orders to HTTP POST. The OrderHttpApi function performed those orders. Now you can test the process of sending orders via Azure Storage Queue directly.

For demo purposes, build a .NET Core console application to send orders to Azure Storage Queue. After creating the .NET Core console project, add the Microsoft.Azure.Storage.Queue library into the project using NuGet.

Next, you declare all the required libraries in your program, as shown here:

```
using System;
using Microsoft.Azure.Storage; // Namespace for
                                   CloudStorageAccount
using Microsoft.Azure.Storage.Queue; // Namespace for Queue
                                      storage types
```

Now you'll write the program to send an order. Define your order data in JSON format. You can write this code:

```
class Program
{
    static void Main(string[] args)
    {
        string order = @"
            {
                'productname':'product ABC',
                'price': 2.55,
                'quantity': 3,
                'buyer':'zahra'
            }
        ";
```

Open Azure Storage Queue using the CloudStorageAccount object and passing its connection string. You can get a connection string from the Azure Storage dashboard. You can see a sample of a connection string in Figure 7-6.

After connecting to Azure Storage, open Azure Storage Queue using `CloudQueueClient` and set your queue name to `order-queue`. Call `CreateIfNotExists()` to create the `order-queue` queue if it is not available. The following is the sample code:

```
string storageConnection = "<connection string-azure
storage queue>";
CloudStorageAccount storageAccount =
CloudStorageAccount.Parse(storageConnection);

Console.Write("Connnectting to Azure Storage
Queue.....");
CloudQueueClient qc = storageAccount.
CreateCloudQueueClient();
CloudQueue queue = qc.GetQueueReference("order-queue");

Console.WriteLine("Connnected to Azure Storage Queue.");
Console.WriteLine("Sending data....");
queue.CreateIfNotExists();
```

You'll send order messages using the `CloudQueueMessage` object. Call the `AddMessage()` method to insert the messages into the queue.

```
CloudQueueMessage message = new CloudQueueMessage(order);
queue.AddMessage(message);

Console.WriteLine("Data was sent to Azure Storage Queue");
Console.ReadLine();
```

Save your project. Compile and run the project. Figure 7-10 shows some program output from your project.

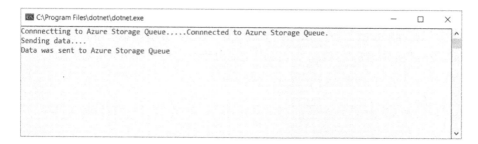

Figure 7-10. *Executing the .NET console application to send orders*

You can verify your order by opening Azure SQL Database. Then, you can perform a query to display the FuncOrder table. Figure 7-11 shows your order data.

Figure 7-11. *A result of the query to display the FuncOrder table*

Summary

In this chapter, we reviewed what microservices are. You also learned how to build a simple microservice with Azure. Various Azure resources were integrated into your project. In the next chapter, you will focus on how to build IoT telemetry by applying Azure Functions projects.

CHAPTER 8

IoT Telemetry System

Developers can use the Internet of Things (IoT) to expand their business. There are various ways to use the IoT with your existing applications. Specifically, you can use Azure Functions to monitor and automate IoT devices. In this chapter, you'll explore how to work with the IoT platform and Azure Functions.

The following topics are covered in this chapter:

- Introduction to the IoT telemetry system

- How to integrate IoT telemetry and Azure Functions

- How to build Azure Functions projects for the IoT

Introducing the IoT Telemetry System

Nowadays, IoT technology drives various industry sectors. There are many platforms for developing IoT applications today such as the Raspberry Pi, Arduino, Beaglebone, and ESP32. You can monitor using IoT devices in some places such as temperature, humidity, and air quality, and obtain real-time data from those devices.

Figure 8-1 shows a general model of an IoT device. There are four components in an IoT device: the microcontroller unit (MCU), sensor, actuator, and network. The MCU is responsible for controlling all I/O processing in the IoT system. The sensor is used to detect physical objects such as temperature and humidity and convert them in digital forms. The

© Agus Kurniawan, Wely Lau 2019
A. Kurniawan and W. Lau, *Practical Azure Functions*,
https://doi.org/10.1007/978-1-4842-5067-9_8

actuator is applied if you want to perform actions such as turning on LEDs and motors. The network module is used to communicate with other systems, for instance, WiFi and Bluetooth.

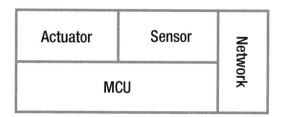

Figure 8-1. *A basic model of an Internet of Thing device*

The IoT telemetry system is one of the IoT systems that senses physical objects or actuates something and then sends the data to a particular server. Most IoT telemetry systems can send massive amounts of data to servers. This system uses various network stacks to exchange data between IoT devices and servers.

In this chapter, you'll explore how to access Azure Functions from the IoT telemetry system.

Integrating IoT Telemetry and Azure Functions

Microsoft provides an Azure solution to enable you to work with various platforms including the IoT. To communicate with Microsoft Azure, you can apply Azure IoT Hub to retrieve data from IoT devices. Azure IoT Hub provides scalable features in order to serve massive data from IoT devices. Azure IoT Hub can manage and monitor your IoT devices. You can find the details of Azure IoT Hub at https://azure.microsoft.com/en-us/services/iot-hub/.

IoT devices can communicate with the Azure back end through Azure IoT Hub with various standard protocols. The following is a list of the supported protocols on Azure IoT Hub:

- HTTPS

- AMQP

- AMQP over WebSockets

- MQTT

- MQTT over WebSockets

Azure Functions can be applied on Azure IoT Hub to listen for incoming data from IoT devices and perform data processing. You can use any program to access Azure Functions. For instance, you can store sensor data in Azure SQL Database, as shown in Figure 8-2.

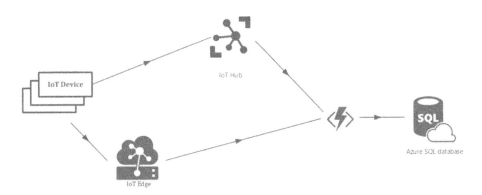

Figure 8-2. *A sample of an integration scenario between IoT devices on the Azure platform*

You can extend your Azure features in your local environment with Azure IoT Edge. You can configure Azure IoT Edge as a gateway device for all your IoT devices. You can deploy your business logic program inside IoT Edge. A benefit of deploying workloads to Azure IoT Edge is that your IoT devices spend less time communicating with the cloud, and these devices even work during certain offline periods.

For further information about Azure IoT Edge, you can visit the official web site at https://azure.microsoft.com/en-in/services/iot-edge/.

IoT Telemetry Data Processing

In this section, you'll learn how to develop IoT telemetry data processing. You can use Azure Functions to perform sensor data processing. All IoT device requests will be handled by Azure IoT Hub. Figure 8-3 shows the demo scenario. All the IoT devices will send sensor data to the Microsoft Azure server through Azure IoT Hub. You'll also prepare Azure Functions to listen for incoming message on Azure IoT Hub. Once Azure Functions receives data, Azure Functions will store that data into Azure SQL Database.

Figure 8-3. *A demo scenario for IoT devices and Azure Functions*

To implement the demo, you should have an active account on Microsoft Azure. Some Azure resources probably will cost money.

Next, you'll create an Azure SQL Database instance.

Creating an Azure SQL Database Instance

Azure SQL Database is one of the Azure services that helps you manage and process your data. If you have experience with SQL Server, you will see that you can get the same functionality with Azure SQL Database. You can work with Azure SQL Database without worrying about infrastructure resources. You can learn more at `https://azure.microsoft.com/en-us/services/sql-database/`.

You can start by creating a database instance with Azure SQL Database. We'll use a small database size for our demo. You can also use an existing Azure SQL Database instance if you have one created. Figure 8-4 shows the Azure SQL Database dashboard. You can see a server called `funcsql` and a database called `azurefuncdb`, as shown in Figure 8-4.

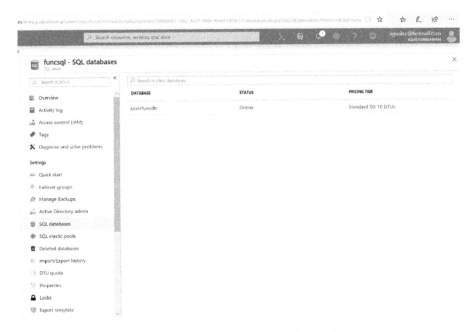

Figure 8-4. *The Azure SQL Database dashboard*

Next, let's create a table for demo purposes using SQL scripting. You'll store two sensor data items: temperature and humidity. The table will be called `Sensor` and will have five columns, as follows.

- `id` is the primary key of the `Sensor` table.

- `deviceid` is the device ID from the IoT device.

- `temperature` is the sensor data for temperature.

- humidity is the sensor data for humidity.

- posted is the date of the received data.

You can create the Sensor table using the following SQL:

```
CREATE TABLE [dbo].[Sensor](
     [id] [int] IDENTITY(1,1) NOT NULL,
     [deviceid] [varchar](15) NOT NULL,
     [temperature] [int] NOT NULL,
     [humidity] [int] NOT NULL,
     [posted] [datetime] NOT NULL,
 CONSTRAINT [PK_Sensor] PRIMARY KEY CLUSTERED
(
     [id] ASC
)WITH (PAD_INDEX = OFF, STATISTICS_NORECOMPUTE = OFF, IGNORE_
DUP_KEY = OFF, ALLOW_ROW_LOCKS = ON, ALLOW_PAGE_LOCKS = ON) ON
[PRIMARY]
) ON [PRIMARY]
GO
```

You can run these scripts in the query editor from the database dashboard in Azure SQL Database. After executing SQL scripts, you can check the table using the query editor, as shown in Figure 8-5. You should see the Sensor table in your database.

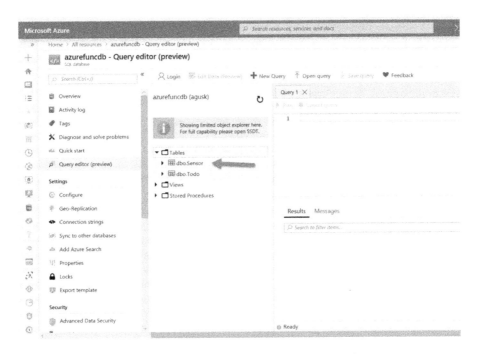

Figure 8-5. *Sensor table created in Azure SQL Database*

Next, you can set up Azure IoT Hub as a bridge between the IoT devices and Microsoft Azure.

Setting Up Azure IoT Hub

Azure IoT Hub is used as a service interface between IoT devices and Microsoft Azure servers. You can use a browser to start setting up Azure IoT Hub by going to `https://portal.azure.com/`.

After selecting the Azure IoT Hub template, you will get a creation form, as shown in Figure 8-6. Fill in all the required fields on this form. Click the "Review + create" button to create a hub with Azure IoT Hub.

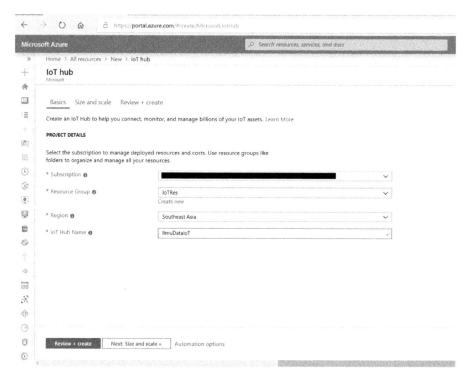

Figure 8-6. _Creating a hub with Azure IoT Hub_

Next, you can create IoT devices on Azure IoT Hub to enable you to communicate with Microsoft Azure. Open your Azure IoT Hub dashboard. Then, open the IoT devices menu on Azure IoT Hub. When you select to create a new IoT device, you will obtain a creation form, as shown in Figure 8-7.

Fill in all the required fields on the form. Select "Symmetric key" for the authentication type. Select the "Auto-generate keys" box. Make sure you enable this device to connect to Azure IoT Hub. When you're done, click the Save button.

After you create an IoT device on Azure IoT Hub, you will see a list of your IoT devices. You can create more IoT devices, but you will probably be charged for additional IoT devices. See Figure 8-8.

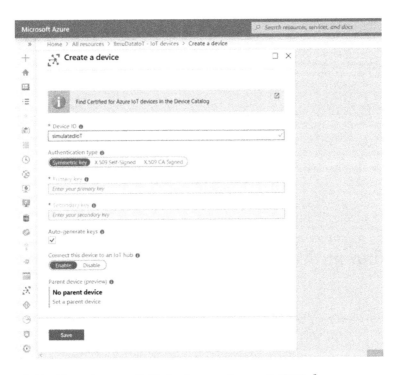

Figure 8-7. *Creating an IoT device on Azure IoT Hub*

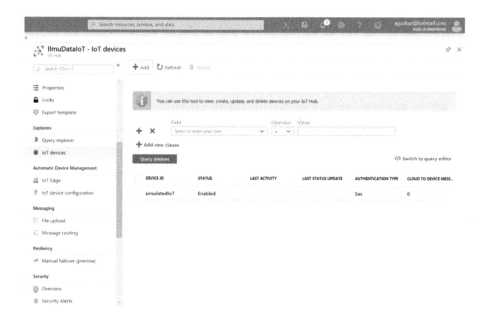

Figure 8-8. *A list of IoT devices on Azure IoT Hub*

Next, you'll build an Azure Functions project to listen for incoming data on Azure IoT Hub.

Creating an Azure Functions Project for the IoT

You can develop an Azure Functions program using the Azure web editor and Visual Studio. You also can create functions in Azure Functions with Azure CLI. In this section, you'll develop functions using Visual Studio 2019.

Start creating an Azure Functions project by selecting the Azure Functions template. Then select the IoT Hub trigger. Figure 8-9 shows the project template for Azure Functions. You can set up a storage account for your project and set up a trigger path with message/iotsensor. Fill in the project name, for instance, **IoTFunctions**. After filling in all the project fields, click the OK button.

You will get some code for your Azure Functions project. Before writing any additional code, you need to add the prerequisite libraries. Add the System.Data.SqlClient and Newtonsoft.Json libraries to your project through NuGet.

Figure 8-9. *Creating Azure Functions functions with an IoT Hub trigger*

The program scenario is to listen for the IoT Hub trigger on the messages/iotsensor path. You will receive a message from IoT devices in the JSON format with the following format:

```
{
    "deviceid": "<deviceid>",
    "temperature":"<temperature>",
    "humidity":"<humidity>"
}
```

You encode this JSON message and convert as a Sensor object via the deserialization process by calling the JsonConvert.DeserializeObject() method. This method is part of the Newtonsoft.Json library. After you obtain the Sensor object, Azure Functions will store it in Azure SQL Database.

The Sensor object holds the device ID and sensor data such as the temperature and humidity. You can define the Sensor object in the Sensor.cs file. The following is the Sensor object implementation:

```
using System;
using System.Collections.Generic;
using System.Text;

namespace IoTFunctions
{
    public class Sensor
    {
        public string DeviceId { set; get; }
        public int Temperature { set; get; }
        public int Humidity { set; get; }

    }
}
```

You can store the Sensor object in Azure SQL Database. Define your own database object, called AzureSQLDB, and call the InsertSensor() method to store the data in the database on Azure SQL Database.

The following is the Azure Functions code implementation:

```
[FunctionName("IoTHubData")]
public static void Run([IoTHubTrigger("messages/iotsensor",
Connection = "IoTHubTriggerConnection")]EventData message,
ILogger log)
{
    log.LogInformation($"C# IoT Hub trigger function processed
    a message: {Encoding.UTF8.GetString(message.Body.Array)}");

    if (message.Body.Array.Length > 0)
    {
        // save into database
        var json = Encoding.UTF8.GetString(message.Body);
```

```
    Sensor sensor = JsonConvert.DeserializeObject<Sensor>(json);
    AzureSQLDB.InsertSensor(sensor);
  }
}
```

The AzureSQLDB object applies ADO.NET objects to manipulate data for SQL Server. You define the InsertSensor() method to store data into Azure SQL Database. You can use the SQLCommand object to execute the INSERT query to store the database by calling the ExecuteNonQuery() method.

```
public static bool InsertSensor(Sensor sensor)
{
    string db = Environment.GetEnvironmentVariable("azure_sql");

    try
    {
        using (SqlConnection conn = new SqlConnection(db))
        {
            conn.Open();
            var text = "INSERT INTO [Sensor](deviceid,temperatu
            re,humidity,posted) " +
                "VALUES(@deviceid,@temperature,@humidity,getdate())";

            using (SqlCommand cmd = new SqlCommand(text, conn))
            {
                cmd.Parameters.Add(new SqlParameter
                ("@deviceid", sensor.DeviceId));
                cmd.Parameters.Add(new SqlParameter
                ("@temperature", sensor.Temperature));
                cmd.Parameters.Add(new SqlParameter
                ("@humidity", sensor.Humidity));
```

```
                cmd.ExecuteNonQuery();

            }
        }
    }
    catch (Exception)
    {
        return false;
    }

    return true;
}
```

You can obtain a connection string for Azure SQL Database from the azure_sql setting. You also pass IoTHubTriggerConnection as the endpoint connection string for Azure IoT Hub. You can define the azure_sql and IoTHubTriggerConnection settings when publishing Azure Functions to Microsoft Azure.

You can also configure the project settings in the local.settings.json file. Define the azure_sql and IoTHubTriggerConnection settings, as shown here:

```
{
  "IsEncrypted": false,
  "Values": {
    "IoTHubTriggerConnection": "<INSERT_ENDPOINT_IOT_HUB>",
    "AzureWebJobsStorage": "<INSERT_AZURE_STORAGE",
    "FUNCTIONS_WORKER_RUNTIME": "dotnet"
  }
}
```

You have developed an Azure Functions project using Visual Studio. Next, you will publish the Azure Functions project.

Publishing an Azure Functions Project

Publishing an Azure Functions project with Visual Studio is easy. Right-click the Azure Functions project and then select the Publish menu. You can publish your project by logging in with your existing Azure account or importing the Azure Functions profile file from Azure Functions.

On the publishing form on Visual Studio, you should configure a connection string for IoT Hub, as shown in Figure 8-10. This connection string consists of endpoint settings from Azure IoT Hub. Fill in your IoT Hub endpoint for the IoTHubTriggerConnection value, as shown in Figure 8-10.

You can obtain the Azure IoT Hub endpoint from the Azure IoT Hub dashboard. You can open the built-in endpoints menu, as shown in Figure 8-11. Copy the value of the Event Hub – Compatible endpoint into IoTHubTriggerConnection from Figure 8-10.

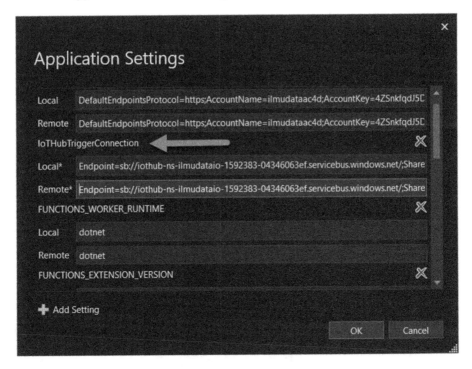

Figure 8-10. *Configuring an IoT Hub trigger connection*

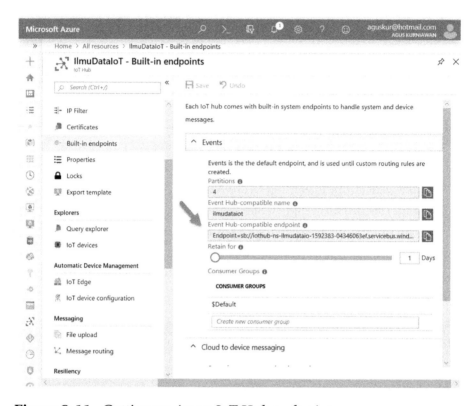

Figure 8-11. *Getting an Azure IoT Hub endpoint*

Next, you can configure a connection string for Azure SQL Database. You already defined the azure_sql setting for your project. You can get the database connection string from Azure SQL Database. Copy the connection string and then paste it into azure_sql in the remote section, as shown in Figure 8-12. When you're done, click the OK button to save these publishing settings.

After you've saved these settings, you can see your function show up in the Azure Functions dashboard. Next, you will test your function.

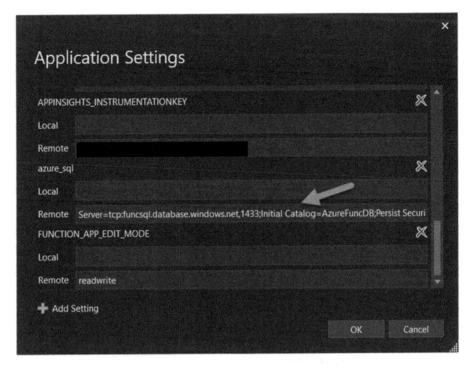

Figure 8-12. *Configuring a database connection for Azure SQL Database*

Testing Your Azure Functions Projects

Azure Functions provides testing tools through the Azure web tool. You can open your Azure Functions projects in the Azure Functions dashboard. Click the Test tab so you can see the testing tools, as shown in Figure 8-13. For this demo, you're sending sensor dummy data in JSON format. You can write this JSON data on the request body:

```
{
    "deviceid": "simulated dev",
    "temperature":"123",
    "humidity":"12"
}
```

You can click the Run button to execute this tool. Technically, you will see verbose messages during testing in the Logs window, as shown in Figure 8-13. You also can see response messages from the Azure Functions server in the Logs window.

Figure 8-13. *Testing Azure Functions from the Azure Functions web tool*

After sending data to Azure Functions, you can verify your data. Open your database in Azure SQL Database. Then, perform a SQL query to see your data. You should see your data that was sent from the web test tool. Figure 8-14 shows your result data in Azure SQL Database.

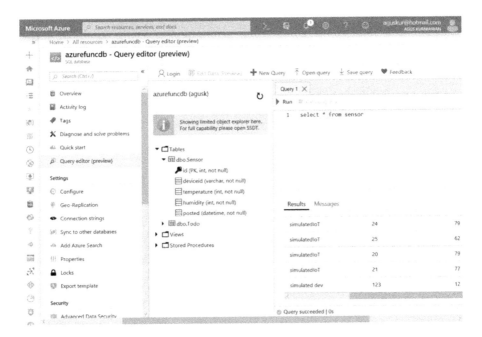

Figure 8-14. *Displaying sensor data using the query editor in Azure SQL Database*

Next, you will develop an IoT program to access Azure Functions.

Developing an IoT Program

You have developed an Azure Functions program and already uploaded it to Microsoft Azure. You also tested the Azure Functions program using the web test tool from Azure Functions. Now you'll develop a program for the IoT platform.

Microsoft has provided SDK libraries for IoT platforms. Currently, Azure IoT SDK libraries are available as follows:

- Azure IoT SDK for C, `https://github.com/Azure/azure-iot-sdk-c`

- Azure IoT SDK for Python, `https://github.com/Azure/azure-iot-sdk-python`

195

- Azure IoT SDK for Node.js, `https://github.com/Azure/azure-iot-sdk-node`

- Azure IoT SDK for .NET, `https://github.com/Azure/azure-iot-sdk-csharp`

- Azure IoT SDK for Java, `https://github.com/Azure/azure-iot-sdk-java`

You can check your IoT devices to see whether these SDK libraries have support for your IoT platform at `https://catalog.azureiotsolutions.com/alldevices`.

For this demo, we'll show how to develop an IoT program using .NET Core. This program can run on an IoT platform with Windows and Linux. For this simple scenario, you'll send random sensor data to Azure IoT Hub. Since this program uses .NET Core, this program can run on your computer for testing purposes.

First, your IoT device or computer needs .NET Core installed on it for testing. If you haven't installed it yet, you can download and install .NET Core at `https://dotnet.microsoft.com/download`.

You can creating the .NET Core program using the `dotnet` command. Type this command on your terminal:

```
$ dotnet new console -o SimulatedIoT
$ cd SimulatedIoT/
```

Then, you'll add the Azure IoT SDK for .NET to your project. Type these commands:

```
$ dotnet add package Microsoft.Azure.Devices.Client --version
1.20.1
$ dotnet restore
```

Now you can write your program. You'll write the code in a `Program.cs` file.

First, declare all the required libraries in your project. You can include the Azure IoT SDK in your program.

```
using System;
using Microsoft.Azure.Devices.Client;
using Newtonsoft.Json;
using System.Text;
using System.Threading.Tasks;
```

You can define a connection string for IoT Hub and the DeviceClient object. Put your connection string for your registered IoT device in Azure IoT Hub. You already registered your IoT device in the "{You device connection string here}" section.

```
class Program
{
        private static DeviceClient deviceClient;
        private readonly static string connectionString =
        "{Your device connection string here}";
```

Open your IoT device in Azure IoT Hub. Then, copy the connection string value from IoT Hub, as shown in Figure 8-15.

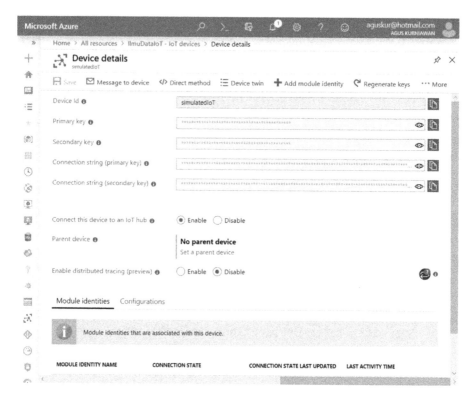

Figure 8-15. *Getting a connection string from an IoT device*

Next, create the SendDeviceToCloudMessagesAsync() method to perform a loop for sending messages to Azure IoT Hub. You can generate random values for temperature and humidity.

```
private static async void SendDeviceToCloudMessagesAsync()
{
    // Initial telemetry values
    double minTemperature = 20;
    double minHumidity = 60;
    Random rand = new Random();

    while (true)
    {
```

```
int currentTemperature = Convert.ToInt32
(minTemperature + rand.NextDouble() * 15);
int currentHumidity = Convert.
ToInt32(minHumidity + rand.NextDouble() * 20);
```

Now construct the sensor data in JSON format. Then, perform serialization for JSON objects using the JsonConvert.SerializeObject() method. To send messages to Azure IoT Hub, you can call the SendEventAsync() method from the DeviceClient object.

```
var sensor = new
{
    DeviceId = "simulatedIoT",
    Temperature = currentTemperature,
    Humidity = currentHumidity
};
var messageString = JsonConvert.SerializeObject(sensor);
var message = new Message(Encoding.ASCII.
GetBytes(messageString));

await deviceClient.SendEventAsync(message);
Console.WriteLine("{0} > Sending message: {1}", DateTime.Now,
messageString);

await Task.Delay(15000);
```

Now instantiate the DeviceClient object by calling the CreateFromConnectionString() method and passing the device connection string. You can also set MQTT as the protocol.

```
private static void Main(string[] args)
{
    Console.WriteLine("Simulated device is running. Ctrl-C to
    exit.\n");
```

```
deviceClient = DeviceClient.CreateFromConnectionString
(connectionString, TransportType.Mqtt);
SendDeviceToCloudMessagesAsync();
Console.ReadLine();
}
```

Save this program. Now you can run this program by typing this command:

```
$ dotnet run
```

This program will send messages to Azure IoT Hub. Figure 8-16 shows some program output.

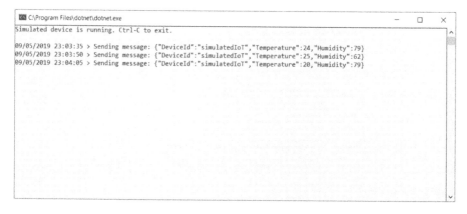

Figure 8-16. *A sample of the program output from a simulated IoT device*

You can verify your sent messages in Azure SQL Database using the query editor tool, as shown in Figure 8-17.

Figure 8-17. *Verifying data in Azure SQL Database*

IoT Telemetry with the Arduino MKR1000

We have shown you how to test your IoT Hub and Azure Functions program using a simulated IoT device. Now we'll show you how to test your program using an Arduino board. Not all Arduino modules can be used to connect to Microsoft Azure. One of the Arduino boards that works is the Arduino MKR1000. This board has already been tested for Microsoft Azure.

The Arduino MKR10000 board can connect a network through a WiFi module and also works with an SSL network. The Arduino MKR10000 board consists of the ATSAMW25 module with the SAMD21 Cortex-M0+, WINC1500 WiFi, and ECC508 CryptoAuthentication modules. For further information about the Arduino MKR10000 board, you can visit the official web site at `https://store.arduino.cc/arduino-mkr1000`.

To simulate sensor data, you can use the DHT22 sensor module that consists of the temperature and humidity sensors. You can find this sensor module easily in your local electronics store. Figure 8-18 shows the DHT22 sensor module's pin layout. The DHT22 sensor module can work with 3.3V and 5V voltages.

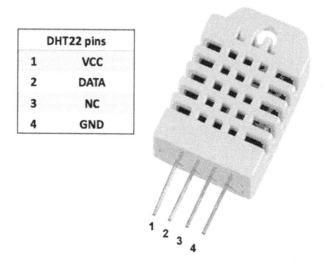

DHT22 pins	
1	VCC
2	DATA
3	NC
4	GND

Figure 8-18. *DHT22 pin layout*

Next, you will perform the hardware wiring for the demo.

Hardware Wiring

In this section, you'll perform the hardware wiring before you develop a program for Arduino. You can connect DHT22 to the Arduino MKR1000 with the following wiring:

- The DHT VCC pin is connected to the Arduino MKR1000 VCC pin.

- The DHT GND pin is connected to the Arduino MKR1000 GND pin.

- The DHT Data pin is connected to the Arduino MKR1000 digital D7 pin.

You can see this hardware wiring in Figure 8-19.

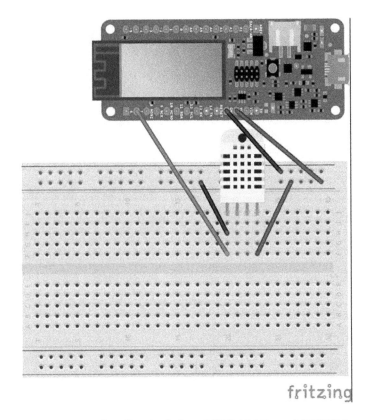

Figure 8-19. *Wiring for the Arduino MKR1000 and DHT22*

Next, you will see how to develop a sketch program using the
Arduino software.

Installing and Configuring the Arduino Software

You can build a sketch program using Arduino. We recommend you use
the latest version of the Arduino software. You can download this software
at http://arduino.cc/en/Main/Software. This tool is available for the
Windows, macOS, and Linux platforms.

After installing the Arduino software, you need to install the Arduino SAMD boards by Arduino to enable to work with the Arduino MKR1000. You can install it by selecting Tools ➤ Board ➤ Boards Manager. After clicking this menu, you should see a Boards Manager dialog. Search for *Arduino SAMD Boards by Arduino*. Install these boards. After they're installed, you should see your Arduino MKR1000 in the Arduino board list. To perform this task, your computer should be connected to the Internet.

You also should install some libraries to enable you to work with DHT22 and Azure IoT Hub. You can install these libraries via the Manage Libraries dialog. You can open this dialog by clicking Sketch ➤ Include Library ➤ Manage Libraries. In the dialog, search for and install the following libraries:

- WiFi101
- RTCZero
- AzureIoT
- DHT Sensor Library
- Adafruit Unified Sensor Lib

Your computer should be connected to the Internet so you can download and install these libraries.

Next, you'll develop a sketch program using the Arduino software.

Writing a Sketch Program

In this section, you'll learn how to develop a program for the Arduino MKR1000. This program will perform sensing through the DHT22 sensor module to obtain the current temperature and humidity. Then, you'll send this sensor data to Azure IoT Hub.

Create a new sketch program and name the project name
ArduinoAzureIoT.ino. You'll also use the ArduinoAzureIoT.c and
ArduinoAzureIoT.h files to manage Azure IoT Hub. First you'll work on the
ArduinoAzureIoT.ino file.

You can declare your required libraries and set the SSID name and
SSID key to connect to the existing WiFi. Change these values in your WiFi
settings:

```
#include "DHT.h"
#include <WiFi101.h>
#include "ArduinoAzureIoT.h"

#define DHTPIN 7      // Digital pin D7 connected to the DHT sensor
char ssid[] = "[wifi-ssid]";      //  your network SSID (name)
char pass[] = "[wifi-ssid key]"; // your network password (use
                                 for WPA, or use as key for WEP)
int status = WL_IDLE_STATUS;
```

You can also configure the Serial object with a baud rate of 9600 and
configure the DHT object with the DHT22 model type data pin on the D7
digital pin.

```
#define DHTTYPE DHT22    // DHT 22  (AM2302), AM2321
DHT dht(DHTPIN, DHTTYPE);

void setup() {
  Serial.begin(9600);
  Serial.println(F("Azure IoT and DHT Demo"));

  // check for the presence of the shield :
  if (WiFi.status() == WL_NO_SHIELD) {
    Serial.println("WiFi shield not present");
    // don't continue:
    while (true);
  }
```

```
// attempt to connect to Wifi network:
while (status != WL_CONNECTED) {
  Serial.print("Attempting to connect to SSID: ");
  Serial.println(ssid);
  // Connect to WPA/WPA2 network. Change this line if using
  open or WEP network:
  status = WiFi.begin(ssid, pass);

  if (status != WL_CONNECTED) {
    // wait 10 seconds for connection:
    delay(10000);
  }
}
Serial.println("Connected to wifi");

dht.begin();
}
```

In the looping function, loop(), you can read the temperature and humidity via the DHT22 module. Then, you send this data to Azure IoT Hub by calling the azureiot_http_run() function that is declared on the ArduinoAzureIoT.c and ArduinoAzureIoT.h files.

```
void loop() {
  delay(20000);

  int h = dht.readHumidity();
  int t = dht.readTemperature();

  if(h==0 || t==0) {
    Serial.println(F("Failed to read from DHT sensor!"));
    return;
  }
```

```
Serial.print(F("Humidity: "));
Serial.print(h);
Serial.print(F("%  Temperature: "));
Serial.print(t);
Serial.println(F("°C "));

Serial.println("Sending data to Azure IoT");
azureiot_http_run(t,h);
}
```

You implement the azureiot_http_run() function on the
ArduinoAzureIoT.c and ArduinoAzureIoT.h files. These files are
a modified program sample from the Azure IoT libraries. In the
ArduinoAzureIoT.c file, you should change your connectionString value
to the connection string from your registered IoT device on Azure IoT Hub.

```
static const char* connectionString = "[device connection string]";
static int callbackCounter;
static int is_done;
```

Inside your azureiot_http_run() function, you construct sensor data
in JSON format. Then, you send it to Azure IoT Hub.

```
sprintf_s(msgText, sizeof(msgText), "{\"deviceId\": \"AR
DUINOMKR1000\",\"temperature\": %d,\"humidity\": %d}",
temperature,humidity);
if ((messages.messageHandle = IoTHubMessage_
CreateFromByteArray((const unsigned char*)msgText,
strlen(msgText))) == NULL)
{
    (void)printf("ERROR: iotHubMessageHandle is NULL!\r\n");
}
```

You can see our complete program in Figure 8-20.

Figure 8-20. *Sketch program on the Arduino software*

Next, you'll learn how to configure an SSL certificate on the Arduino MKR1000.

Updating an SSL Certificate for Azure IoT Hub

Before you upload your program onto your Arduino MKR1000 board, you should update and configure your SSL certificate from your Azure IoT Hub. If not, you will get errors because of the SSL certification.

First upload the FirmwareUpdater program into the Arduino MKR1000. You can get this program from the program samples by selecting File ➤ Examples ➤ WiFi101 ➤ FirmwareUpdater. After uploading the FirmwareUpdater program into the Arduino MKR1000, your board is ready for the updated firmware for the WiFi module.

You can update the WiFi firmware on the Arduino MKR1000 by clicking Tools ➤ WiFi1011 / WiFiNINA Firmware/Certificate Updater. After clicking the menu, you should get the dialog shown in Figure 8-21.

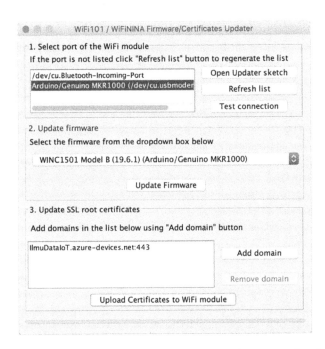

Figure 8-21. *Updating the firmware and configuring the SSL certificate*

Select your Arduino MKR1000 port. Then, select the firmware version you want. I recommend you choose the latest version of the firmware. Then, add your Azure IoT Hub domain by clicking the "Add domain" button. Fill in your Azure IoT Hub domain. You can get this information on the Azure IoT Hub dashboard.

Click the "Upload Certification to WiFi module" button to update the firmware and SSL certificate. Make sure you disconnect UART accesses on the Arduino MKR1000.

After updating the firmware and the SSL certificate, you are ready to upload your program and test it.

Testing the Program

Now you can compile and upload the sketch program. You can perform these tasks on the Arduino software by clicking the Verify and Upload icons. After uploading the program, you can see the program output by opening the Serial Monitor tool by clicking Tools ➤ Serial Monitor.

You should see your program output that sensed the temperature and humidity from DHT22. Then, the program sends this sensor data to Azure IoT Hub. You can see our program output in Figure 8-22.

Figure 8-22. Program output in the Serial tool

You can verify your data was sent to Azure IoT Hub by opening Azure SQL Database. You can perform a query to display all the data in the Sensor table. Figure 8-23 shows the sensor data that was sent by the Arduino MKR1000.

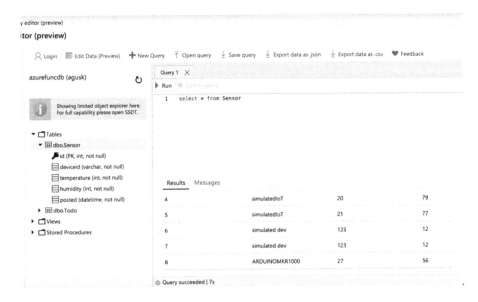

Figure 8-23. *Verifying data on Azure SQL Database*

Summary

In this chapter, you learned how to access Azure Functions from IoT devices. You also already have developed a simple project with implementing Azure Functions, Azure IoT Hub, and Azure SQL Database. In the next chapter, you will focus on how to work with Azure monitoring and Application Insights.

CHAPTER 9

Monitoring Azure Functions with Application Insights

Monitoring is an essential part of the software development lifecycle. Without proper monitoring, it would be challenging to improve an application by identifying bugs or increasing the performance. You can monitor Azure Functions using Application Insights.

Since Application Insights is a big topic, we will not be able to cover every single detail of it in this chapter. Rather, you will learn about telemetry and how to monitor Azure Functions with Application Insights in this chapter.

Introduction to Application Insights

Application Insights, often called App Insights, is an application performance monitoring (APM) solution that is part of the Azure platform. Figure 9-1 illustrates how Application Insights works.

© Agus Kurniawan, Wely Lau 2019
A. Kurniawan and W. Lau, *Practical Azure Functions*,
https://doi.org/10.1007/978-1-4842-5067-9_9

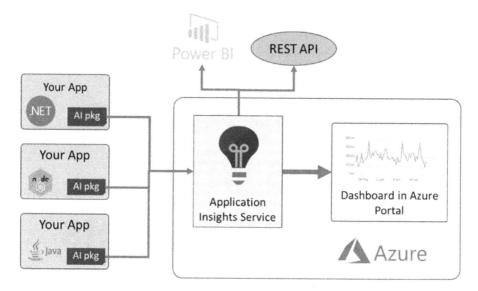

Figure 9-1. *App Insights architecture*

App Insights works by embedding a tiny instrumentation package in your application.

App Insights supports various platforms and programming languages (such as .NET, NodeJS, Java, PHP, etc.) through the official Application Insights team support and through community support. For more details about the platform support, please visit https://docs.microsoft.com/en-us/azure/azure-monitor/app/platforms.

The App Insights package will periodically instrument your application and ingest the telemetry data to the backend Application Insights service. The Application Insights service will then perform the necessary operations before displaying the reports to the dashboard. A typical report includes the following:

- Request rates, response times, failure rates

- Exceptions and errors

- Page views and performance

- Diagnostic trace logs

You can learn more about the dashboard details at `https://docs.microsoft.com/en-us/azure/azure-monitor/app/app-insights-overview#what-does-application-insights-monitor`. Other advanced reports such as smart detection and alerts leverage artificial intelligence (AI) to alert when there is something outside of the usual pattern.

You learned about building a microservices architecture with Azure Functions in Chapter 7. Related to this, App Insights is capable of monitoring and instrumenting not just your app's code but also some of the external services that your app connects to. This capability is known as *distributed tracing*. You can learn more about it at `https://docs.microsoft.com/en-us/azure/azure-monitor/app/distributed-tracing`.

In addition to viewing the dashboard in the Azure portal, you can use Power BI to connect to App Insights or export the data through the REST API.

Using an analogy, think of App Insights as an X-ray machine that will help you diagnose what's wrong in your body so that the doctor can cure you accordingly. Similarly, you use App Insights to instrument your app. When you find out what is causing the failure or performance issue, then you can rectify it.

Provisioning Application Insights

Let's begin this section by provisioning an App Insights instance. To do that, navigate to the Azure portal and click "+ Create a resource." Choose Application Insights in the Developer Tools category, as shown in Figure 9-2.

Figure 9-2. *Creating an App Insights instance*

Like with other Azure services, you'll need to choose your preferred subscription and resource group in the project details. Provide the name and choose your preferred region where your Azure Functions app is located. In the example shown in Figure 9-3, the App Insights instance is named **AIForAzureFunctions**. Then click "Review + create" to complete the creation process.

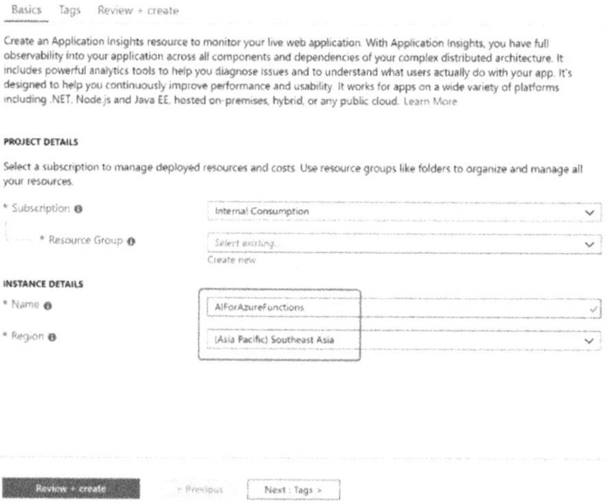

Figure 9-3. *Naming the App Insights instance*

After a few moments, you will be able to see the Application Insights Overview tab, as shown in Figure 9-4. The instrumentation key, as shown in the main section, serves as an identifier so that the App Insights package sends the telemetry information to the App Insights back-end service. On the left side, you'll see several menus that you can investigate and monitor with App Insights. We will discuss some of them later in the chapter.

Figure 9-4. *Application Insights Overview tab*

Integrating Application Insights to Azure Functions

There are a few ways to integrate App Insights into Azure Functions. If you are creating a few Azure Functions apps, you will have the option to also create an App Insights instance during provisioning, as we discussed earlier.

What you're going to do now is to integrate the App Insights instance that you just created to Azure Functions. To do that, choose the Function App menu in your Azure portal and then pick a function app (ideally without an App Insights instance configured on it), as shown in Figure 9-5.

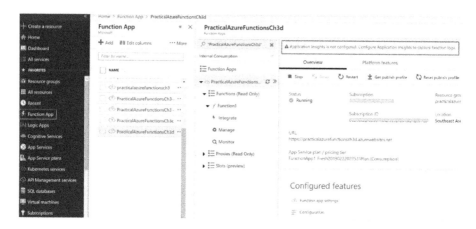

Figure 9-5. *Integrating App Insights to Azure Functions*

You will see a warning message in the App Insights Overview blade indicating "Application Insights is not configured. Configure Application Insights to capture function logs" if the Azure function app does not have any App Insights instance configured. Simply click that warning message to launch the App Insights blade, as shown in Figure 9-6.

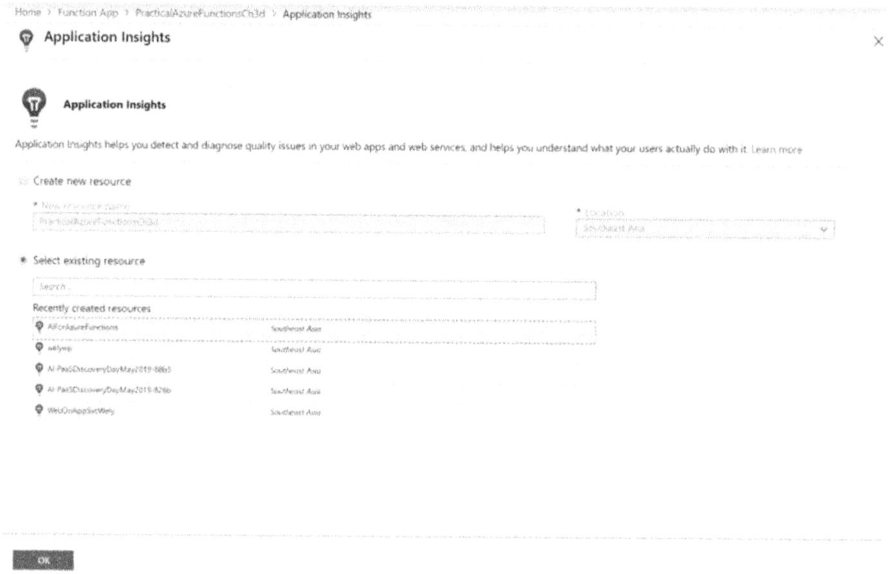

Figure 9-6. *App Insights blade in the Azure portal*

The next step is to choose your preferred App Insights instance and then click OK. Once the configuration has been successfully performed, you will be able to see the Live Stream dashboard, as shown in Figure 9-7. As you can see, there isn't any request at all.

Figure 9-7. *Live Stream dashboard in App Insight*

You are going to generate some load to verify whether the integration has been successfully done. If your function is using the HTTP trigger, you can simply invoke the URL using a browser or an event with a tool such as Postman.

Navigate back to the Live Stream dashboard, and you should see that the line chart is being updated in real time just like in Figure 9-8. This is because of the traffic that you just generated.

Figure 9-8. *App Insights' Live Stream dashboard with traffic*

Detecting Failures and Errors in Azure Functions with App Insights

We all know that errors are inevitable in the software development world. Unfortunately, because not all errors are reported by end users, the administrator or application developer will not be able to fix them.

In this section, you will learn how App Insights can help application developers discover failures and errors in Azure Functions.

Simulating Failures in Azure Functions

In this section, you'll develop a function to perform the division operation of two parameters. You can add this function on an existing Visual Studio project or create a new project. Listing 9-1 shows the function's code.

Listing 9-1. Code for Division Operation Function

```
using System;
using System.IO;
using System.Threading.Tasks;
using Microsoft.AspNetCore.Mvc;
using Microsoft.Azure.WebJobs;
using Microsoft.Azure.WebJobs.Extensions.Http;
using Microsoft.AspNetCore.Http;
using Microsoft.Extensions.Logging;
using Newtonsoft.Json;

namespace PracticalAzureFunctionsCh9
{
    public static class Division
    {
        [FunctionName("Division")]
        public static async Task<IActionResult> Run(
            [HttpTrigger(AuthorizationLevel.Anonymous, "get",
            "post", Route = null)] HttpRequest req,
            ILogger log)
        {
            log.LogInformation("C# HTTP trigger function
            processed a request.");

            string a = req.Query["a"];
            string b = req.Query["b"];

            string requestBody = await new StreamReader(req.
            Body).ReadToEndAsync();
            dynamic data = JsonConvert.DeserializeObject
            (requestBody);
            a = a ?? data?.a;
            b = b ?? data?.b;
```

```
            decimal result = 0;
            result = decimal.Parse(a) / decimal.Parse(b);
            string response = $"{a} / {b} = {result}";
            log.LogInformation(response);

            return (ActionResult)new OkObjectResult(response);
        }
    }
}
```

You may notice that the code in Listing 9-1 has not been properly written. For example, there is no format validation to accept a number. Another issue is the possibility of a division-by-zero exception.

Let's deploy this function to a function app with App Insights.

Once the function has been deployed on Azure, let's start to invoke the function URL from the browser with the valid parameter's value to make sure that your function runs properly. To do that, pass parameter a with a value of 5 and pass parameter b with a value of 2. As expected, you get a response of 5 / 2 = 2.5, as displayed in Figure 9-9.

Figure 9-9. *Division operation with the valid parameter*

This time you'll generate a failure by passing in an invalid format. To do that, let's set the parameter a with the value of 8 and set b with a value of x. As shown in Figure 9-10, you get an HTTP 500 error response.

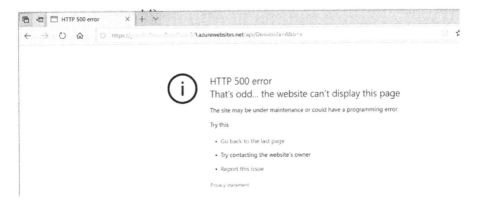

Figure 9-10. *HTTP 500 error of format exception*

You are not done yet; let's generate another error now by setting the parameter a with the value 6 and set the parameter b with the value 0. Similar to the previous step, you get another HTTP 500 error, as shown in Figure 9-11.

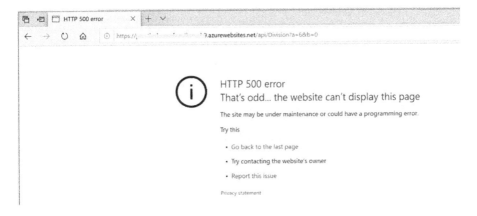

Figure 9-11. *HTTP 500 error of division-by-zero exception*

Viewing Failure Details in App Insights

Since you have already generated some failures, you will be viewing the failure details in App Insights in this section. Typically, you will be able to see data captured in the Live Stream dashboard almost in real time. However, in other App Insights menus, typically you will be able to see the data appear in less than five minutes.

Let's navigate to the Azure portal. Under the App Insights menu, and click Failures, as shown in Figure 9-12.

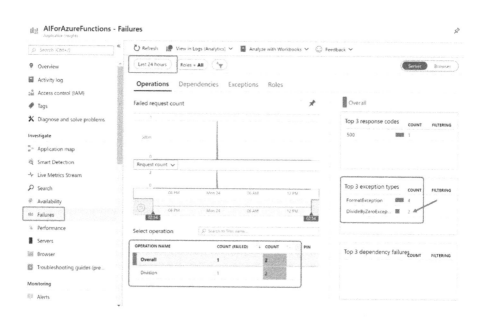

Figure 9-12. *Failures menu in App Insights*

You can filter the time frame by changing the "Last 24 hours" setting to your preferred time frame. You should notice that there's Division operation failures in the bottom section and the exception types for the Division operation on the right side. Click the count for DivideByZeroException to see the details. In our case, we have 2, but your case may differ. Immediately, you should see the failure incident's details such as date and time, as shown in Figure 9-13.

Figure 9-13. *Failure incident details in App Insights*

You can change the sort by date. Click one of the failure incident, and you will see another blade, as shown in Figure 9-14.

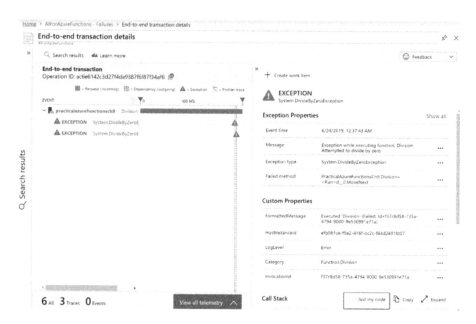

Figure 9-14. *End-to-end transaction details in App Insights' Failures menu*

This provides many more details of the failure incident including the call stack if you scroll the right pane to the lower section. Now select the "Just my code" box in the Call Stack section, and you will be able to see your code. This is where App Insights is really amazing as it tells you which code triggered the `DivideByZeroException`; here it's at line 31, as shown in Figure 9-15. One of the interesting things to note is that you can also create a work item directly on this blade if your App Insights instance is connected to Azure DevOps.

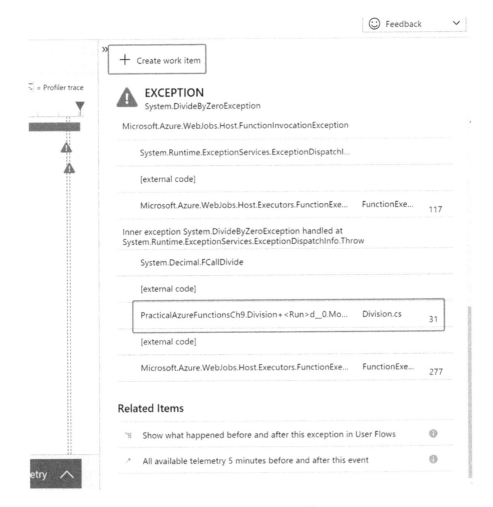

Figure 9-15. *Exception details in App Insights*

Let's check out line 31 in your function code to make sure that it points to the right failure case. Figure 9-16 displays the screenshot of the line 31; you can see we didn't perform any validation of variable b before performing the division operation.

```
29
30      decimal result = 0;
31      result = decimal.Parse(a) / decimal.Parse(b);
32      string response = $"{a} / {b} = {result}";
33      log.LogInformation(response);
```

Figure 9-16. *Code that results in a failure in the function*

Load Testing, Autoscaling, and Real-Time Monitoring

We will be showing an interesting scenario in this section to showcase the combination of three technologies. You will be using an Azure DevOps performance test to perform load testing against Azure Functions. You will then monitor Azure Functions, especially the autoscaling behavior, in real time with App Insights.

Preparing Your Code

To demonstrate this scenario, let's modify the code listing you used earlier. To do that, right-click the Visual Studio project and select Add ➤ New Azure Function, as shown in Figure 9-17.

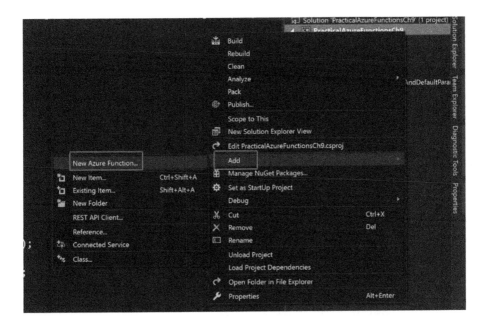

Figure 9-17. *Adding a new function to the Visual Studio project*

Provide the name DivisionWithRandomDelayAndDefaultParameter.
Then add the code shown in Listing 9-2 to your Azure Functions project.

Listing 9-2. Code for Division Operation Function with Random
Params and Errors

```
using System;
using System.IO;
using System.Threading.Tasks;
using Microsoft.AspNetCore.Mvc;
using Microsoft.Azure.WebJobs;
using Microsoft.Azure.WebJobs.Extensions.Http;
using Microsoft.AspNetCore.Http;
using Microsoft.Extensions.Logging;
using Newtonsoft.Json;
using System.Threading;
```

```
namespace PracticalAzureFunctionsCh9
{
    public static class DivisionWithRandomDelayAndDefault
    Parameter
    {
        [FunctionName("DivisionWithRandomDelayAndDefaultParameter")]
        public static async Task<IActionResult> Run(
            [HttpTrigger(AuthorizationLevel.Anonymous, "get",
            "post", Route = null)] HttpRequest req,
            ILogger log)
        {
            log.LogInformation("C# HTTP trigger function
            processed a request.");

            string a = req.Query["a"];
            string b = req.Query["b"];

            string requestBody = await new StreamReader
            (req.Body).ReadToEndAsync();
            dynamic data = JsonConvert.DeserializeObject
            (requestBody);

            a = a ?? data?.a;
            b = b ?? data?.b;

            Random randParam = new Random();
            if (a == null)
                a = randParam.Next(25, 50).ToString();
            if (b == null)
                b = randParam.Next(0, 10).ToString();

            int sleepDelay = 0;
            Random randDelay = new Random();
            sleepDelay = randDelay.Next(0, 10);
```

```
Thread.Sleep(sleepDelay * 1000);

decimal result = 0;
result = decimal.Parse(a) / decimal.Parse(b);
string response = $"{a} / {b} = {result}";
log.LogInformation(response);

return (ActionResult)new OkObjectResult(response);
        }
    }
}
```

You will notice that Listing 9-2 is actually a modified version of Listing 9-1 where you set the value of parameters a and b when they not defined in the query string.

The value of parameter a is filled with a random number between 25 and 49. The value of parameter b is filled with a random number between 0 to 9. This is done intentionally to simulate some cases of a DivisionByZero exception. The listing also has a sleepDelay parameter with a random value between 0 and 9 seconds. The reason for doing this is to generate some delay with Thread.Sleep() so that you can see Azure Functions will provision additional servers for you to handle the other requests.

Publishing to Azure

You can build and publish the code to Azure. Once the code has been successfully published to Azure, let's verify it by simply accessing the URL from a browser. If all goes well, you will see there might be a delay in accessing the URL because of Thread.Sleep(), and you will see the division operation for two values being shown. Obviously, you may see different values from ours, as shown in Figure 9-18.

Figure 9-18. *Accessing division with default values and sleep*

Refresh your browser multiple times to simulate several requests. Now navigate to App Insights and check out the Live Stream dashboard to verify whether the requests you made were captured in App Insights.

Generating the Load with Performance Testing

Moving on, in this section you'll be generating a load for performance testing with Azure DevOps. This can be done either through the Azure portal, Azure DevOps, or even Visual Studio. Of course, you may also choose to use your preferred load testing tools such as JMeter, LoadRunner, Loader.IO, and so on. To streamline the experience, you will be using the Azure portal from the App Insights menu.

Navigate to the Azure portal and look for the App Insights instance that you created earlier in the chapter; then scroll down until you see Performance Testing under the Configure section, as shown in Figure 9-19.

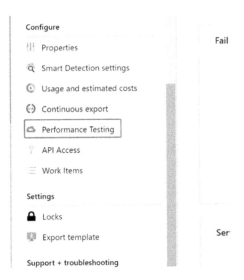

Figure 9-19. *Choosing Performance Testing in App Insights*

When the Performance Testing blade opens, you will see the performance testing history, as shown in Figure 9-20.

Figure 9-20. *Performance testing history in the App Insights menu*

You can choose to change the performance testing configuration with another Azure DevOps account by clicking the Set Organization button.

Or you can click the New button to trigger a new performance test. Once the new performance test blade opens, you can start by choosing the test type, as shown in Figure 9-21.

Figure 9-21. *New performance test*

There are two types of test.

- Manual Test, which simply generates an HTTP request to the URL specified

- Web Test, which is a more advanced mode allowing you to record a scenario and upload it as a `.webtest` file

In this example, choose Manual Test and put the URL of your function in the URL box. In this example, the URL is `https://domain.azurewebsites.net/api/DivisionWithRandomDelayAndDefaultParameter`. Click Done to return to the previous blade.

Give the performance test a name such as **LoadTestingAzureFunction**. You can also choose the data center region where you want the load to be generated from. Subsequently, fill in the user load, which simulates the request. Finally, fill in the duration of the load test in minutes. Figure 9-22 displays the performance test details we specified (1,000 user loads over a period of five minutes). Click "Run test" to complete it.

Figure 9-22. *Adding details to generate the load test*

The Azure portal will bring you back to the performance test history blade, where you will see the state of the load testing initially in Queued. You can click it to see the details of the performance test in another blade, as shown in Figure 9-23.

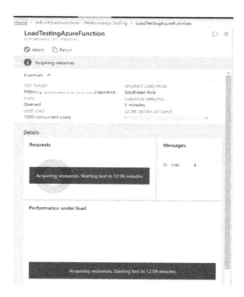

Figure 9-23. *Acquiring resources in the performance test*

As you can tell from the information, Azure DevOps needs some time to acquire the number of resources (load test agent) on the data center region that you defined earlier. In addition to the parameters specified on the load test, the waiting time depends on several factors, such as the data center capacity.

Monitoring the Live Stream Metric During a Performance Test

In just a few moments, you can see that the performance test page turns to In Progress: X %, which indicates that the performance test has started.

Let's immediately open another browser or browser tab to browse to App Insights and then the live stream metric. You can arrange the browser windows side by side, as shown in Figure 9-24.

Figure 9-24. *Side-by-side view: load testing and live stream metric*

The left side shows that the load test is being performed by Azure DevOps through the App Insights menu. The right side shows the live stream metric during the performance test. Notice the number of servers online, which originally was only one instance before the performance test and has now increased to 13. This proves the elasticity and autoscale capabilities of Azure Functions during peak traffic.

Figure 9-25 shows another view after several minutes of running. In fact, the number of servers has increased to 18 in this experiment.

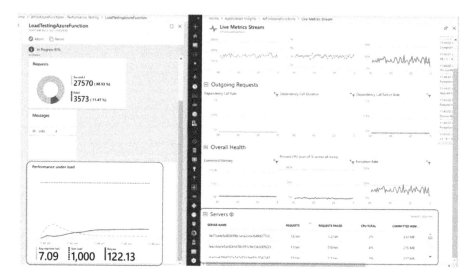

Figure 9-25. *Side-by-side view: load testing and live stream metric, bottom sections*

The lower section on the left side displays the ongoing results of the performance test, including the average response time. The lower section on the right side shows the server's name provisioned along with details such as the number of requests, CPU, and memory consumed.

Cooldown Period and Result of Performance Testing

After the five-minute performance test, Azure Functions will cool down in approximately 15 minutes since there was not that much traffic. During the cooldown period, Azure Functions will gradually scale the number of instances to eventually just 1.

Let's move back to the performance test summary page. Click "Request details," and you will see the request details summary, as shown in Figure 9-26.

Figure 9-26. *Performance test summary and request details*

In addition to the summary page, now that you have more data in App Insights, you can navigate to other App Insights menus for further investigation or to create alerts.

Summary

In this chapter, we introduced App Insights and showed how to integrate it into Azure Functions. You then learned how to use App Insights to detect failures in Azure Functions. During the latter part of the chapter, you combined load testing from Azure DevOps, autoscaling features from Azure Functions, and the live stream metric from App Insights to monitor the performance test in real time.

Index

A, B

AddMessage() method, 163, 173

Android application development
  Android studio, 145
  Azure functions, 150, 151
  data verification, 152
  designing UI, 146
  EditText components, 146
  JSON data, 148
  SDK libraries, 144
  Toast object, 150
  URL, 147

Application insights
  architecture, 213, 214
  Azure functions (*see* Azure function, application insights)
  creative instance, 215, 216
  distributed tracing, 215
  naming, 216
  overview tab, 217
  typical report, 214

Application performance monitoring (APM), 213

Apps dashboard, 12, 13

App Service Plan, 11

Azure function, application insights
  division operation function, 229–231
  failure details
    end-to-end transaction, 225, 226
    exception details, 226, 227
    incident's details, 225
    menu, 224
    result, 227, 228
  failure, simulation
    function's code, 220–222
    HTTP 500 error, 222, 223
    parameter, 222
  live stream dashboard, 219
  new function, 228, 229
  publish, code, 231, 232
  sleepDelay parameter, 231
  testing (*see* Performance testing)
  traffic, 219, 220

Azure functions *vs.* logic apps, 20, 21

azureiot_http_run() function, 206, 207

Azure IoT Hub, 178, 179, 183–186

J, K

L

M

W, X, Y, Z

CPSIA information can be obtained
at www.ICGtesting.com
Printed in the USA
LVHW082111151119
637496LV00007B/70/P

9 781484 250662